Beneath the Dome of ???, in the legendary vaults of Aarok, the treacherous L'Bastin is cloning an army of terrifying super-warriors, to conquer the cosmos. And only YOU, Sky Lord Jang Mistral, élite solar trooper, special agent – and four-armed fighter! – from the sixteenth aeon, can stop him.

Armed with a laser sword and pistol, electro-javelin and spiked buckler, you must journey into the vaults and defeat the evil mastermind. But beware! L'Bastin has set many traps. Monsters, mutants and space brigands lie in wait for the unwary, and success is by no means certain. If you fail, millions will die; if you succeed, you will win a prize almost beyond your wildest dreams!

Two dice, a pencil and an eraser are all you need to embark on this thrilling adventure, which is complete with its elaborate combat system and a score sheet to record your gains and losses.

Many dangers lie ahead and your success is by no means certain. YOU decide which routes to follow, which dangers to risk and which monsters to fight.

Fighting Fantasy Gamebooks

THE WARLOCK OF FIRETOP MOUNTAIN
THE CITADEL OF CHAOS
THE FOREST OF DOOM
STARSHIP TRAVELLER
CITY OF THIEVES
DEATHTRAP DUNGEON
ISLAND OF THE LIZARD KING
SCORPION SWAMP
CAVERNS OF THE SNOW WITCH
HOUSE OF HELL
TALISMAN OF DEATH
SPACE ASSASSIN
FREEWAY FIGHTER
TEMPLE OF TERROR
THE RINGS OF KETHER
SEAS OF BLOOD
APPOINTMENT WITH F.E.A.R.
REBEL PLANET
DEMONS OF THE DEEP
SWORD OF THE SAMURAI
TRIAL OF CHAMPIONS
ROBOT COMMANDO
MASKS OF MAYHEM
CREATURE OF HAVOC
BENEATH NIGHTMARE CASTLE
CRYPT OF THE SORCERER
STAR STRIDER
PHANTOMS OF FEAR
MIDNIGHT ROGUE
CHASMS OF MALICE
BATTLEBLADE WARRIOR
SLAVES OF THE ABYSS
SKY LORD
STEALER OF SOULS
DAGGERS OF DARKNESS
ARMIES OF DEATH
PORTAL OF EVIL
VAULT OF THE VAMPIRE

Steve Jackson's *Sorcery!*

1. The Shamutanti Hills
2. Kharé – Cityport of Traps
3. The Seven Serpents
4. The Crown of Kings

FIGHTING FANTASY – The Introductory Role-playing Game
THE RIDDLING REAVER
OUT OF THE PIT – **Fighting Fantasy Monsters**
TITAN – **The Fighting Fantasy World**

Steve JACKSON AND Ian LIVINGSTONE PRESENT

SKY LORD

by Martin Allen

Illustrated by Tim Sell

PUFFIN BOOKS

Thanks to
Keith, Richard, Andrew, Gail, Cugel, Mum and Dad

PUFFIN BOOKS

Published by the Penguin Group
27 Wrights Lane, London W8 5TZ, England
Viking Penguin Inc., 40 West 23rd Street, New York, New York 10010, USA
Penguin Books Australia Ltd, Ringwood, Victoria, Australia
Penguin Books Canada Ltd, 2801 John Street, Markham, Ontario, Canada L3R 1B4
Penguin Books (NZ) Ltd, 182–190 Wairau Road, Auckland 10, New Zealand

Penguin Books Ltd, Registered Offices: Harmondsworth, Middlesex, England

First published 1988
3 5 7 9 10 8 6 4 2

Concept copyright © Steve Jackson and Ian Livingstone, 1988
Text copyright © Martin Allen, 1988
Illustrations copyright © Tim Sell, 1988
All rights reserved

Printed and bound in Great Britain by
Cox & Wyman Ltd, Reading
Filmset in 11/13 Linotron Palatino by
Rowland Phototypesetting Ltd
Bury St Edmunds, Suffolk

Except in the United States of America,
this book is sold subject to the condition
that it shall not, by way of trade or otherwise,
be lent, re-sold, hired out, or otherwise circulated
without the publisher's prior consent in any form of
binding or cover other than that in which it is
published and without a similar condition
including this condition being imposed
on the subsequent purchaser

CONTENTS

ABOUT YOUR STAR SYSTEM
7
YOUR ABILITIES
11
COMBAT
13
ADVENTURE SHEET
18
SPACE COMBAT SHEET
20
MISSION BACKGROUND
22
COUNTDOWN . . .
29

ABOUT YOUR STAR SYSTEM

You are Sky Lord Jang Mistral, élite solar trooper, special agent – and four-armed humanoid warrior – from the sixteenth aeon.

Your home planet, Ensulina, is just one of countless thousands of worlds inhabiting the famous Holo Faluksh star chain – a dazzling spray of more than one hundred thousand live stars and innumerable planetoids, bordering the Berenices Supergalaxy. Some of these worlds, whether baking in the wild solar flares of near-by suns or wandering the bitterly cold galactic wastes, are only lifeless husks. These are of little value to anyone except the ruthless galactic pirates and space desperadoes who use them for their evil purposes. Yet there exist many other worlds less daunting: with kinder climates and hospitable environments; on many of these a wondrously diverse array of life-forms have established themselves.

Your own race, the Ensulvars, is a blood-mix of two ancient nations: the dawn-time Enzuls, the planet's original inhabitants, and the Ivars, a war clan from Iajax-Green. The Ivars invaded Ensulina during the second aeon, at first defeating and later mixing into the more populous Enzul race. The resulting nation of grey-eyed, four-armed humanoids retained the best traits of their ancestors: the culture and wisdom of the Enzuls, and the courage of the Ivars. As a result, they have been respected and admired by the inhabitants of many other planets in the star system (particularly the two-armed humanoids!) and enjoyed a peaceful existence for many years.

During the twelfth aeon, however, a vast galactic war suddenly broke out: two powerful races, the Fethps (greedy, two-headed reptiloids) and the Deik (large purple molluscoids of unknown origins), always deadly rivals, had secretly amassed mighty armies and space fleets. Simultaneously their armadas stormed across the galaxy at each other, destroying or conquering the planets in their path. The war raged for thousands of years, during which time Ensulina was conquered by the merciless Deik. The Ensulvars were enslaved and forced to produce war machinery for their captors.

Only gradually, following wave upon wave of murderous assaults on each other, did the strength of the Deik and Fethps begin to wane. In the thirteenth aeon the enslaved races of thousands of worlds were sparked to revolution. Led by Ari Skyfarer, a human from Arbitrakt, they rapidly ousted their cruel masters and, employing the weaponry they had previously been forced to build, finally drove both the Deik and Fethps from the star system.

The end of the war signalled the beginning of the Long Peace which has lasted to this day. Ari Skyfarer, the greatest galactic hero, was crowned first Grand Emperor and, in order to maintain a lasting peace, the Council of Star Kings was formed. The council, whose members include the kings of many worlds (including your own King Vaax), usually meets every five hundred days at the Grand Emperor's palace on Arbitrakt. There, the council tries to resolve peacefully any disputes between its member planets and reaffirms its intention to defend its planets from alien threats, galactic pirates and intergalactic invaders. The latter functions are performed by the Emperor's Imperial Guard, or by the heroic solar troopers – of whom you are a member.

On Ensulina, the title of 'lord' is not a birthright, but must be earned in some way. It was your exceptional skill and courage shown when fighting in the ranks of the solar troopers which earned you your first lordship title – that of a Knight of Ensulina – when you were only twenty years old. Since that time your fellow peers, the lords of Ensulina, have often employed you as a special agent, performing hazardous and extremely secret missions to ensure the security of Ensulina and the Friendly Worlds. Because of your accomplishments, you have been honoured with further titles – the latest, that of Sky Baron, being awarded after capturing the murderous Olaf Tharkin and his band of solar cutthroats.

But now you have been summoned to appear before King Vaax and your fellow lords, to be briefed on a new mission: the most perilous, most challenging – and most unusual – adventure of your career. Failure will bring disaster for Ensulina; success will bring you a treasure beyond your wildest dreams . . .

However, before you can receive details of your mission, you must learn how to use your special skills and weapons and your starship, which will assist you during the course of your adventure. You will also require two dice, a pencil and an eraser, to record your scores and equipment gained along the way.

YOUR ABILITIES

Your abilities to fight, withstand damage and escape from tricky situations are determined by your SKILL, STAMINA and LUCK points. On the *Adventure Sheet* on pages **18–19** you will see sections where these attributes are to be recorded. They are obtained as follows:

Roll one die. Add 6 to the result. Enter this total as your SKILL.

Roll two dice. Add 12 to the result. Enter this total as your STAMINA score. If your STAMINA ever reaches zero, then you have been killed.

Roll one die. Add 6 to the result. Enter this total as your LUCK.

Using Luck

From time to time you will be called upon to *Test your Luck*. When this occurs, roll two dice. If the result is *less than or equal to* your current LUCK score, then you have been Lucky. If the result *exceeds* your current LUCK score, then you have been Unlucky.

Each time you *Test your Luck*, you must deduct 1 point from your current LUCK score. Thus the more you use your LUCK, the riskier it becomes. LUCK points may sometimes be restored (you will be told in the relevant paragraph when this is so), but may never exceed your *Initial* score.

Restoring Stamina

During the course of your adventure, you are almost certain to lose STAMINA points. Generally, you may recover these by consuming Provision Tablets at any time other than when engaged in combat or other hostilities. You begin your adventure with 10 Provision Tablets – list these on your *Adventure Sheet*. For each tablet you consume, you will recover 4 points of STAMINA. Note, however, that your STAMINA may never exceed its *Initial* score.

Restoring Skill

There will be occasions during the adventure when you may lose SKILL points, and other occasions when you may gain SKILL points. However, your SKILL may never exceed its *Initial* value.

Money

You also begin your adventure with 10 credits, the most common galactic currency. Add these to your *Adventure Sheet*.

COMBAT

During the course of your adventure you will probably be required to fight in two distinctly different sorts of battles, known as Personal Combat and Combat-Weapon Clashes.

Personal Combat

The rules for Personal Combat are much the same as in other Fighting Fantasy Gamebooks, but with a few minor differences to keep in mind. The basic rules of combat are:

1. Combat is simultaneous. Individual combat is conducted as a series of rounds, in which one combatant will inflict damage on the other.
2. Roll two dice and add your opponent's SKILL score to the roll. This total is your opponent's Attack Strength.
3. Roll two dice again and add your SKILL score to the roll. This total is your Attack Strength.
4. If your opponent's Attack Strength is greater than yours, the opponent has inflicted damage upon you: deduct 2 points from your STAMINA.
5. If your Attack Strength is greater than your opponent's, you have inflicted damage upon your opponent: deduct 2 points from your opponent's STAMINA.

6. If both Attack Strengths are equal, both attacks have missed. Start the next combat round from step 2 above.
7. Continue this combat until either your opponent's or your own STAMINA is reduced to zero (death).

In cases where you are instructed to fight more than one opponent, fight only the first listed. If you defeat this opponent, go on to fight the second listed, and so on.

Using Luck in Combat

On certain pages of the book you will be told to *Test your Luck*, and you will find out the consequences of being Lucky or Unlucky. However, in personal combat (but *not* in combat-weapon clashes), you always have the option of using your LUCK either to inflict a more serious wound on an opponent you have just wounded, or to minimize the effects of a wound you have just received.

If you have just wounded your opponent, you may *Test your Luck* as described above. If you are Lucky, you have inflicted a severe wound and may subtract an *extra* 2 points from its STAMINA score. If you are Unlucky, however, the wound turns out to be a mere graze and you must restore 1 point to your opponent's STAMINA (i.e. instead of scoring the normal 2 points of damage, you have now scored only 1).

If your opponent has just wounded you, you may *Test your Luck* to try to minimize the wound. If you are Lucky, you have managed to avoid the full force of the blow: restore 1 STAMINA point (i.e. instead of losing 2 points, you lose only 1). If you are Unlucky, you have taken a more serious wound and must subtract 1 *extra* STAMINA point.

Remember that you must subtract 1 point from your LUCK score each time you *Test your Luck*.

Combat-Weapon Clashes

When you fight an opponent who has a RATING and numbers for LASERS and SHIELDS listed in the text, then you are involved in a Combat-Weapon Clash. Unlike Personal Combat, these encounters usually involve fighting between sophisticated combat vehicles, one of which is always piloted by yourself.

You have already attained a good proficiency, or RATING, in piloting many combat vehicles. Roll one die to determine your RATING; if you roll 1, 2 or 3 your RATING equals 3; if you roll 4, 5 or 6 your RATING equals 4. Then enter the result in the RATING box on your *Adventure Sheet*.

The basic rules for Combat-Weapon Clashes are:

1. Combat-Weapon Clashes, unlike Personal Combat, are *not* simultaneous. To determine which craft (yours or your opponent's) will fire first, compare your RATING to your opponent's RATING. (Your RATING will not be given in the text, of course; refer each time to your *Adventure Sheet*.) If your RATING number is greater than your opponent's, you will shoot first; otherwise, your opponent will shoot first. The one who fires first in combat is the *Attacker*, the other is the *Defender*.
2. Roll one die. If the result is *less than or equal to* the number of LASERS on the Attacker's combat weapon, he has scored a hit: deduct 2 SHIELDS from the Defender's combat weapon.
3. Now the Defender retaliates. Roll one die again.

If the result is *less than* the number of LASERS on the Defender's craft, he has scored a hit: deduct 2 SHIELDS from the Attacker's combat weapon.
4. Continue the combat from step 2 above, until either your or your opponent's SHIELDS are reduced to zero (death).
5. If you win the combat, then you may reinstate the SHIELDS of your combat weapon to their value before the combat began, since the energy banks quickly regenerate after a combat. In addition, if your opponent's RATING number was *greater* than your own RATING, you may increase your RATING by 1 point.

At the beginning of your adventure, you are equipped with a starship, the *Starspray*. A plan of the *Starspray* is shown on your *Space Combat Sheet* on pages 20–21. Whenever you are involved in a Combat-Weapon Clash using the *Starspray*, you may use the starship plan to record hits against your ship (simply cross off the SHIELD boxes to record hits). Then, if you win the combat, you may return your SHIELDS to their strength before the combat began by simply erasing the crosses.

ADVENTURE SHEET

SKILL *Initial* *Skill =*	STAMINA *Initial* *Stamina =*	LUCK *Initial* *Luck =*

RATING	CREDITS *Initial = 10*	OXYGEN SUPPLY POINTS *Initial = 10*

NOTES AND ITEMS

ALIEN ENCOUNTER BOXES

Skill = Stamina =	Skill = Stamina =	Skill = Stamina =
Skill = Stamina =	Skill = Stamina =	Skill = Stamina =
Skill = Stamina =	Skill = Stamina =	Skill = Stamina =
Skill = Stamina =	Skill = Stamina =	Skill = Stamina =

SPACE COMBAT SHEET
STARSHIP: *STARSPRAY*
DATA: 4 HIGH POWER LASERS L
       12 FORCE SHIELD PODS S

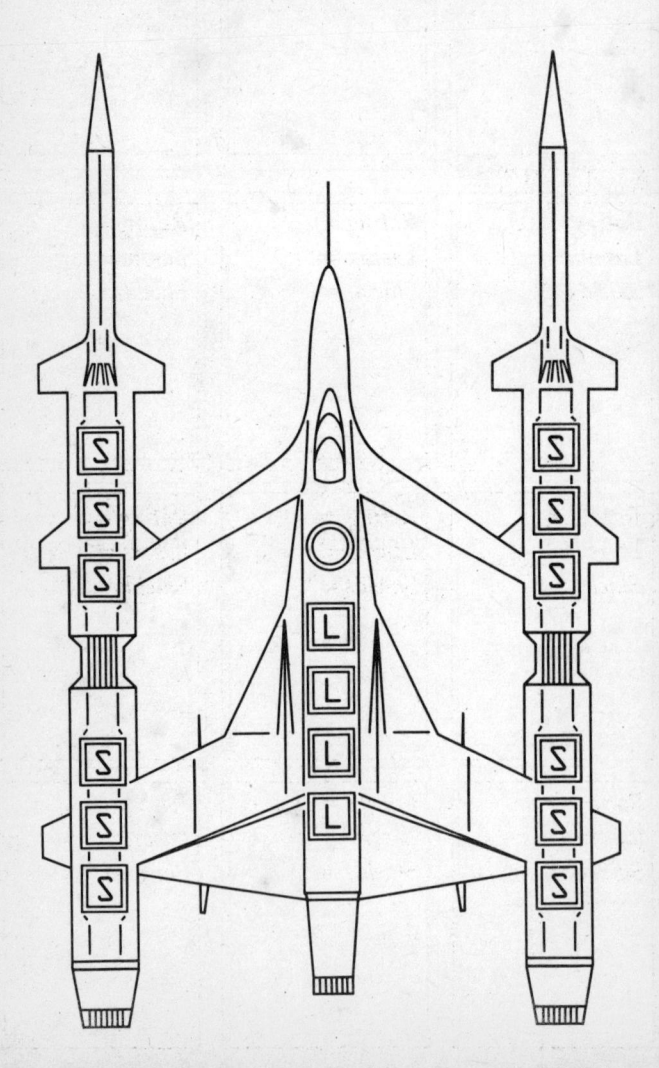

COMBAT WEAPON ENCOUNTERS
YOUR VEHICLES:

Rating =	Rating =	Rating =
Lasers =	Lasers =	Lasers =
Shields =	Shields =	Shields =

ALIENS:

Rating =	Rating =	Rating =
Lasers =	Lasers =	Lasers =
Shields =	Shields =	Shields =

Rating =	Rating =	Rating =
Lasers =	Lasers =	Lasers =
Shields =	Shields =	Shields =

Rating =	Rating =	Rating =
Lasers =	Lasers =	Lasers =
Shields =	Shields =	Shields =

MISSION BACKGROUND

The name 'L'Bastin', even if only whispered, would certainly cause the faces of the Ensulvar palace staff to flush with anger. From poor King Vaax, however, it would bring an uncontrollable outburst of such ferocity that the employment of a large hypodermic tranquillizer might well be advisable, for his own well-being!

Of course, it has not always been like this. In fact there was a time when L'Bastin, the now infamous galactic renegade and scourge of Ensulina, had enjoyed a much more friendly relationship with your king. In those days, he had occupied a position of authority and prestige. As Vaax' major-domo, his responsibilities had included the employment and supervision of the king's entire household staff – a job which he handled with due skill and diligence for a number of years.

But then he took up a new hobby – cybernetics and genetic engineering – and his attitude changed drastically. In order to pursue his leisure-time activity, L'Bastin had to build a laboratory and equip it with many varieties of cloning, fusing and transforming hardware, and then buy important scientific publications. Of course, all of this required a large amount of money. After running up sizeable debts, L'Bastin approached King Vaax and begged for an increase in his modest wage; following years of faithful service, he considered that he had earned it. The artful Vaax, however, steadfastly refused, claiming that, in the interests of the national economy, virtually no one in Ensulina had been allowed a pay rise for over two hundred years. To grant one to L'Bastin, he argued, 'could set a dangerous precedent, which would undermine the entire economy, to the mutual disbenefit of all'.

L'Bastin, who believed that these were merely the words of a stingy ruler, was infuriated. The economy, as everyone well knew, had never been in better shape! In retaliation, the crafty courtier devised a scheme whereby he could obtain the money he needed for his creditors while simultaneously causing his tight-fisted monarch some inconvenience. The scheme went thus: on the pretext of maintaining exceptionally high standards of behaviour among the palace catering staff, L'Bastin began dismissing the stewards for trivial misdemeanours. Upon receiving their marching orders, these unfortunates were immediately escorted from the premises and informed that, if they were ever to return, they would face a speedy execution! In their place, the wily L'Bastin substituted creations from his own laboratory; these obliged their master faithfully by investing their weekly wages with him!

After his initial successes with the stewards, L'Bastin set about dealing with the other palace staff with equal fervour. The fact that many of his creations resembled dismissed staff was no mere coincidence, and within a surprisingly short space of time he was receiving pay packets from chefs, chauffeurs, guards, groundsmen, and even the king's personal advisers and henchmen, all without arousing the least suspicion.

With his supplementary income thus assured, L'Bastin got himself released from debt. For a while he contented himself with engineering whimsical creatures for his own amusement: the spider-fly and the gigantic fanged armadillo-bodied rhinoceros in particular were sources of great satisfaction to him! Indeed, at that time the chambers beneath his manor-house fairly teemed with bizarre livestock. Eventually, however, L'Bastin grew dissatisfied. The *ultimate*, the most rewarding experience, he concluded, could be derived only from the creation of the perfect life-form – whatever *that* was. He grew determined to find out, although accomplishing the task would consume a considerable amount of money, and require the acquisition of some extremely sophisticated equipment indeed . . .

Purchasing a brand-new metamorphosal hydrolizer 'special' required an enormous financial outlay – even more than his dishonest tactics had afforded him thus far. Another money-making scheme was required: L'Bastin ordered one of his henchmen to pilfer and then pawn a number of palace artworks. Several antique porcelain vases were first to go, followed by a crystal statuette (the personal property of the king), and a cosmoscope entitled 'Birth of a Star'. Since by now there were few 'reals' left among the palace staff, L'Bastin believed that the thefts would go unnoticed. And they would have, too, if he had chosen someone other than his creation, Ben Frumpet, to carry out the crime.

One day, when Ben was in a local pawnbroker's establishment, haggling over a suitable price for the stolen cosmoscope, in walked the *real* Ben Frumpet, his identical namesake. (The real Frumpet, one-time head chef, had been unemployed since his dismissal from the palace, and had gone to the broker to hock his gold watch.) The real Frumpet suddenly twigged the situation and, after a brief protest, he stunned his facsimile and dragged it off to the local constabulary.

Thus, L'Bastin's conniving schemes were finally exposed; his henchmen were weeded out and the original staff reinstated. For his crimes, the king punished L'Bastin severely. After a not-too-lengthy trial, Vaax sacked L'Bastin from his post, ordering his laboratory to be demolished and his manor-house confiscated. The former major-domo was to be thrown into the streets!

But L'Bastin, seething with anger, had other ideas. Clearly, he would soon be forced to leave Ensulina to continue his work – but first he planned a final mordant joke upon the king, now his sworn enemy! Disguising himself as a famous cosmetic surgeon, L'Bastin visited the king's wife, Broomhilda, offering her 'beautifying treatment' free of charge; naturally, Broomhilda accepted. Contrary to his promised beautification, however, the despicable mastermind played an awful prank upon her: while she was upon the operating table, he carried out certain 'modifications' to her, extending her nose by ten inches, enlarging her eyes to the size of small saucers and discolouring them (one red, one green) and, worst of all, grafting a large pineapple to her scalp (sadly, a process not entirely reversible!). This cruel act was discovered only when the bandages were removed a week later – and by then L'Bastin had fled the planet.

Despite the generous reward offered for his capture, L'Bastin has remained hidden for years. During the past week, however, a bounty hunter has landed, bringing startling news to Ensulina. He claims to have tracked L'Bastin to Aarok, a man-built fortress-world orbiting the galactic rim. Aarok was abandoned by its makers centuries ago, following a massive radiation spill. Since then it has become the abode of dreadful galactic cut-throats and varieties of abhorrent creatures, as well as many eccentric recluses. The bounty hunter captured and interrogated a mutant, obtaining from it the following information: deep within the vaults of Aarok, L'Bastin has long been experimenting on the local livestock, breeding and refining their better traits, until recently he developed the 'perfect' life-form he sought. Rumours say that they are terrifying dog-headed superwarriors with brutal strength and electrifying speed, calling themselves 'Prefectas'. L'Bastin is busily cloning an army of them, which he will unleash upon the galaxy. Particularly harsh treatment is planned for King Vaax and the Ensulvars!

Fortress Aarok bristles with automatic missiles, lasers and pulsers, and is surrounded by energy shields and vacuum mines: at present it is impregnable to invasion by a large force. But, as the bounty hunter has proved, a solitary craft may be able to pass through the screens, and land, undetected. Once down, this lone invader would need to destroy the planet's defence centre, located beneath the Dome of Marvels, deep within the planet's interior. Only by this means would an invasion fleet be able to land safely. The task ahead is fraught with danger, and only Ensulina's most skilful agent – you – will have any chance of succeeding. Knowing that failure may cost billions of lives, still you have accepted the mission. If you succeed, however, the fabulous man-built world will at last be decontaminated and repopulated – and *you* will be crowned its sovereign ruler!

Now the time has come for you to leave your home planet, Ensulina, and travel to distant Aarok in your starship.

Turn to paragraph **1**

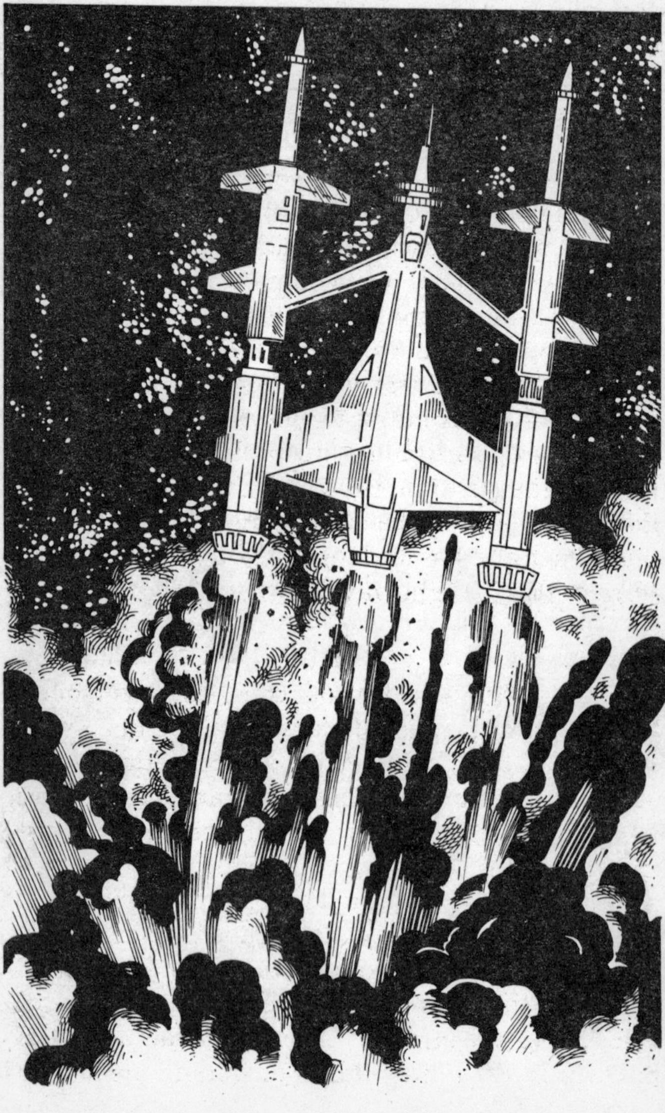

1

After a short rest, you gather your equipment and board your spaceship, the *Starspray*, where you begin a quick, pre-programmed countdown sequence. Ten, nine . . . the energy banks hum; eight, seven, six . . . thrusters ignite, your seat judders; five, four, three . . . pulsers roar, a loudspeaker announces: 'Dimension hop imminent!', two, one . . . Bang! Your home planet disappears from the vidi-screen; the sky is black and starless. You have entered a warp-lane. From this lane, you must steer the *Starspray* into another dimension: one more suitable for rapid galactic travel to Aarok. Your best opportunities are probably time–space travel in the 4th dimension, or light–space travel in the 6th dimension. Each has advantages over the other; each also has its dangers. Will you time-travel (turn to **164**), or light-travel (turn to **15**)?

2

You feel giddy and close your eyes. When you open them, you find yourself standing alone in a cylindrical tube, ten feet high and four feet wide. As you study it, touching its walls, the transmat cylinder gently revolves, revealing a thin, rectangular opening. Stepping through, you alight upon a long-spanned causeway located several miles above the floor of an immense, ovoid chamber. Around you, in mid-air, elegant diamond, snowflake and cuboid lanterns drift lazily past, mingling rich tinctures of ochre, magenta and puce. Slender canals and rainbow rivers with fine bridges of shining metal leap through spaces, straining between horizons. Deserted manors, museums, libraries and temples of fanciful design adjoin causeways, or hover amidst spectacular floating gardens, wondrous sculptures and sparkling holograms. You have entered Vault 5, the principal domicile of Old Aarok. Radiation levels here are still quite high. Miles away to the north-west, you discern the colourful Dome of Marvels, its base veiled in mist. The planet's defence centre is installed in Vault 6, directly beneath the dome. Unfortunately, your causeway runs south-west to north-east, passing high to the right of your target. You deliberate for some time before setting off. Will you march along the causeway north-east (turn to **318**), or south-west (turn to **202**)?

3
All circle-shaped tiles change colour: orange to green, green to blue, blue to orange. Now you may step on tile E2 (turn to **350**), or tile D3 (turn to **156**), or tile C2 (turn to **278**).

4

Rather than making for the entrance, you foolishly decide to drill your way into the dome. After breaking open the globe, you strap the drill-helmet to your head and ram it into the dome's metal crust. Unluckily, the shell is harder than you had anticipated; eventually the drill becomes jammed. Now, instead of the drill-head revolving, *your* head begins to spin, twisting the rest of you with it! In a moment your body becomes detached from the helmet and you skittle away, over the rooftop and down towards the dome's entrance. Your adventure is over.

5

The old man leads you on. He is Marsatu, 'An Ensulvarian *by assemblage*,' he says, 'and a trader by repute.' Pondering the meaning of his words, you climb a ramp and, skirting a terrace, arrive at the entrance to his hovering mansion. Marsatu rings a chime and, after a pause, the door is opened by an absurd, trout-headed footman, dressed in a scarlet tunic. Marsatu introduces him to you: 'This is Bok, my servant. Bok, we will be having a distinguished visitor for supper. Fetch our best porcelain tankards, and warm the mead!' Bok scuttles off while Marsatu leads you via a maze of oak-panelled passages to a roomy, octagonal parlour. Here, you make polite conversation until Bok returns, carrying two large bowls. One of these is filled with a green liquid, the other with a blue liquid. Marsatu gestures vaguely to you. Will you drink the green liquid (turn to **155**), or the blue liquid (turn to **61**)?

6

Brac's laser blasts a hole through your buckler and body armour, into your shoulder. Luckily the armour absorbed much of the energy. Deduct 4 points from your STAMINA and 1 point from your SKILL. Brac prepares to fire again. Turn to **158**.

7

Unsure as to which way you should go, you finally turn down a small passage and follow it towards a bend. At the corner ahead is a high, triangular door while, just past the door, a large perspex plaque is set on the passage floor. You will have to tread on the plaque if you wish to continue your journey along the passage. Will you open the door (turn to **74**), or make your way along the passage (turn to **161**)?

8

Your craft darts and weaves into range, and a burst of laser fire splashes the Valioog ship. As you might have expected, the craft has powerful shields, and the attack fails. As you veer away, your cabin is scorched by a heat-gun. Reduce your SHIELDS by 2 points *permanently*, and deduct 1 point from your STAMINA. Now you may operate anti-detector systems (turn to 70), an image intensifier scanscope (turn to 215), or computer-scan the enemy (turn to 163).

9

You enter the space station's sports complex: a wide concrete area containing dumb-bells, parallel bars, tennis courts, a space-ball arena and much, much more. Momentarily distracted by the equipment here, you decide to test your prowess at one of the games. Will you try your skill at snooker (turn to 77), or space-ball (turn to 113)?.

10

The Deik's shell opens a crack and releases a long, rubbery stalk. At the end of this appendage, the Deik first forms a small eyeball, which swivels menacingly towards you. After a moment the eye collapses and remoulds itself into a trumpet-like mouth. 'Oi, four-arms!' it says to you. 'I haven't seen you here before. What do ya' think ya'r up to? Come 'ere!' Will you:

Pretend to be a cretin, and answer the Deik stupidly?	Turn to 139
Act like a rogue, and answer him arrogantly?	Turn to 36
Obey the Deik's command, and walk across to him?	Turn to 51

11

Soon you are detected by the massive *Grand Archipelago*, which roars forward to accept your challenge. At this moment, your computers flash with the following tactical data:

Starspray: Pitch −16 ... Roll +22 ... Yaw −31 ...
Enemy: Pitch +35 ... Roll +60 ... Yaw +13 ...
Relative Distance 7000 ... Speed 1000 ...

Based on this information, will you:

Maintain speed and course?	Turn to 205
Accelerate to 2000, maintain course?	Turn to 360
Maintain speed, yaw −10?	Turn to 107

12

The new Glip turns the red ring one segment clockwise, and charges across the rings to attack you on your mechanical grasshopper.

	RATING	LASERS	SHIELDS
GLIP	4	3	8
GRASSHOPPER	−	4	10

If you win, a third Glip appears on the recently vacated spot on the red ring. Scuttlebug then decides not to rotate the blue ring, so he is blocked. Mutant rotates the yellow ring one segment anticlockwise, and his phase ends. The fourth and final move begins, and you still need to defeat a Scuttlebug to win. Will you rotate the red ring one segment clockwise (turn to 303), or two segments anticlockwise (turn to 361)?

13

Inside the cabinet is a live Prefecta, lying on a mattress of tough, green hair. Obviously it had not anticipated your sudden appearance: it offers no defence. You beat it insensible and throw it into the mechanical hopper, where it slides from view. Then, just in time, you enter the cabinet and pull the doors shut. Outside there is considerable commotion as the Prefectas search the laboratory without success. Eventually they depart towards the air-tube and Vault 6; you decide to stay put and rest for a while. Now the only voices you can hear are those of the three Yappies. 'The mixture's ready!' you hear Zap say after a while. 'Now, pump it into the vats.' For several hours all is silence; in fact, you are just relaxing into a peaceful slumber when the unusual green mattress suddenly turns upon you: many of its hairs expand to enormous thickness, clamping your arms and legs. Other hairs remain thin, but grow longer, wriggling up your nostrils and down your throat. You are almost smothered by them when, strangely, the hairs retract to normal size. Immediately there is a wild shriek from outside: 'Something's gone wrong! Zap, Brag; eyeball this!' Several screams later, the cabinet doors are flung wide open by Zap. 'You!' he cries accusingly. 'Why, oh, why did yar enter the mouldin' cabinet? See what you've done? We're as good as dead, man!' Looking out, you see what is troubling them: the bench-tops have all been removed to reveal the wooden incubation vats in which the Prefectas are grown. However, instead of gazing upon hundreds of quickly maturing Prefectas, you see hundreds of fast-growing facsimiles of yourself! Of course, when they are ready they will still behave like Prefectas (albeit over-salted ones), because of the unique chemical mix used in their preparation. Brag waves his arms in despair. 'Yeah, the first batch won't feel good about this! Can't think for the rest o' yar, but I'm vaccin' me way out o' here, before they find out.' Brag rushes from the laboratory, closely followed by his two comrades. You muse for a while; deciding that the cabinet is still the safest place to be, you swing its doors shut again. After a few more minutes, you hear the new Prefectas struggling from their tubs. They are even arguing among one another as they wander in a group out of the laboratory, towards the air-tube. The fun is about to begin! Turn to **187**.

14

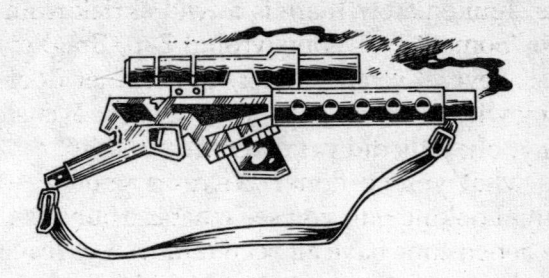

The enemy ship explodes in a spectacular ball of heat and light. You manoeuvre the *Starspray* through the debris, probing for survivors and spoils. One item which immediately attracts your attention is a droid: a spindly chrome robot of dwarfish proportions. Its three faces have frozen in terror and it clutches frantically to a buckled wing-slat. A droid may be a useful acquisition for your mission; you pick it up in a mechanical grabber and pop it into your ship's hold. You also spot a curious device of iron tubes, glass rods and slate cubes. Although you are unaware of its function, it looks very high-tech, so you scoop it up also. Turn to **311**.

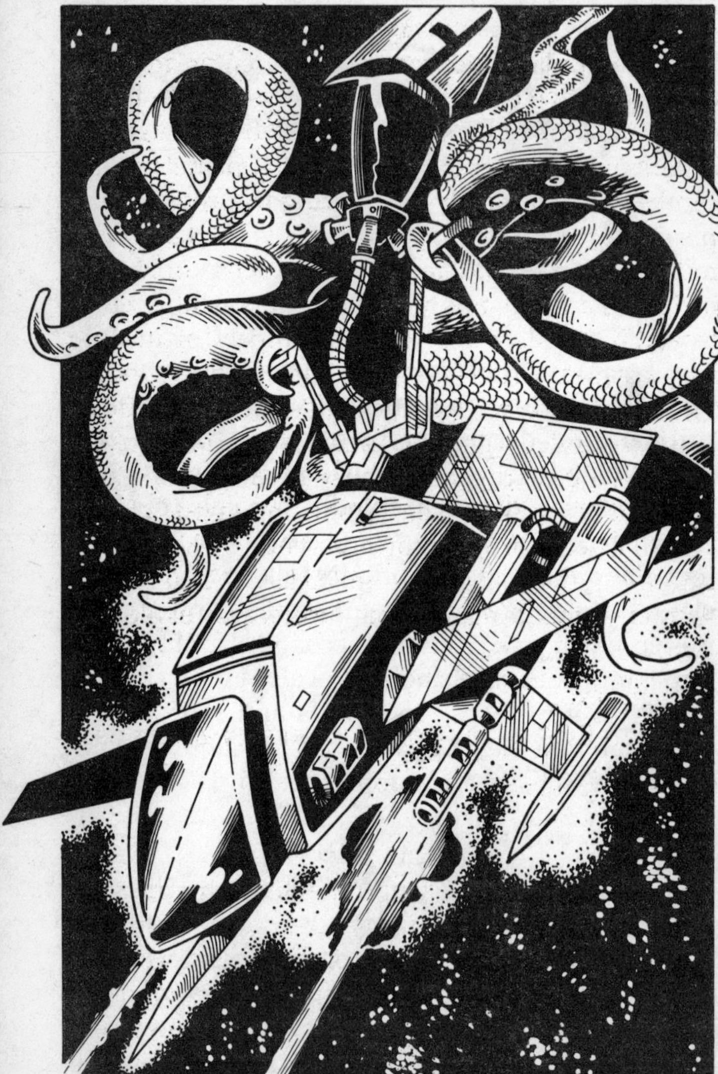

15

You manipulate the controls and enter the 6th dimension in a blaze of colour and sound. In lightwarp, the universe you know is folded upon itself in a complex colour pattern, so that any planet or star can be reached merely by entering the appropriate portion of the colour spectrum. It will take only a millionth of a second 'real time' to reach Aarok – but in less than half this time your spaceship's electrostatic shields blaze with the impact of incoming missiles. From a higher dimension, a huge red rocket scooter appears. Its rider, a scruffy, black-tendrilled creature, wears a scarlet choker: the tell-tale mark of a Fahbad Redneck, a gang of galactic thrill-seekers from the 33rd plane. The Redneck throttles towards you, making rude gestures and laughing manically. You must defend yourself against his lasers and explosive ram.

FAHBAD
  REDNECK   RATING 4 LASERS 5 SHIELDS 8

If you win, turn to **41**.

16

You follow Zud and his machine through a maze of corridors, rooms and tunnels before, eventually, you arrive at his chamber: a small laboratory with racks laden with bottles, flasks, mirrors and many indescribable gizmos. Without a word, Zud manoeuvres his craft to an old oak desk, where he uses a long-armed grabber to extract a curious metal tube from the top drawer. The tube is sealed; at one end there is a keyhole. 'Here, take a closer look!' cries Zud, and the grabber thrusts the cylinder straight at your chest. Horrifyingly, it merges painlessly into your flesh; only the keyhole is visible! (Add Zud's cylinder to your *Adventure Sheet*.) Zud is bleating with delight. 'Fell right into my little trap!' he snaps. 'Oh, don't worry, the tube's quite harmless, really it is – though what's inside it may not be! Ha, ha!' After a long-winded cackle, Zud continues. 'I will explain: the tube is made of titanium, it's specially coated and is virtually indestructible. Have no fears about losing it – it will not easily come loose, I assure you! Within it resides my stout little friend, Gnasha. Unfortunately, I've spoilt Gnasha by feeding him too much good food; now he will eat only the choicest metals and, occasionally, flesh. He has quite an appetite; if you listen carefully, no doubt you will hear him gnawing at the end of the tube – the end closest to your heart.' Zud pauses long enough for you to verify his statement, before he continues. 'How long it will take him to chew his way out, I am not sure; it could be hours, or . . .' This is too much for you to handle! Furious, do you tug at the cylinder's exposed end with all your might (turn to **79**), or hurl a flask of acid at the despicable Zud (turn to **102**)?

17

As you reach the terminal building, you are spotted by two guards: bony-faced creatures with powerful meta-blasters.

	SKILL	STAMINA
BUG-EYED CORPORAL	7	8
SNOUT-NOSED TROOPER	6	10

If you win, will you hide the bodies in a nearby ventilator shaft (turn to **309**), or immediately enter the tubeway station and take an air-carriage into the city (turn to **397**)?

18

There is a squeal as the Brutes are splashed with the acid and hop away in pain. Unluckily, you too are splashed – roll one die and deduct that number of points from your STAMINA. If you are still alive, then, if you have any ointbush leaves, turn to **97**; otherwise, turn to **221**.

19

There is a loud blast from the reeds, and you are hit by molten steel, glass and plastic. Deduct 3 points from your STAMINA. With no other choice, you surrender. Turn to **252**.

20

'Righty-ho then, matey!' he sneers. 'But I'll not have you joining Captain Big-ears' ship.' With that, two burly Rogues climb overboard and attack with laser-knives and crude matchlocks.

	SKILL	STAMINA
BALD-HEADED ROGUE	7	10
FEATHER-FACED ROGUE	6	10

If you win, turn to 370.

21

Matters are finally sorted out. Marsatu, as payment for his fare, must eventually hand over to Jym all his credits. However, since you cannot pay, Jym makes a diabolical suggestion. 'I will take you wherever you wish, if you will entertain me for a while. Can you juggle?' he quips. 'No. Dance or sing? No. Well, never mind. I have invented a special kind of entertainment for non-payers. Just follow me.' Jym leads both of you with your machines into his tower. In a circular hall on level X, you find the Roundabout. The giant snaps his fingers and, apparently from nowhere, three armoured ruffians appear: a Glip, a one-eyed Scuttlebug, and an exotic yellow Aarok Mutant. The Glip, dressed head-to-toe in red battle-armour, is mounted on a six-legged red animal; he is holding a stout electro-lance. His companions wield an assortment of javelins, lasers, and inertia-less chains. Jym faces you. 'You must play a game of Galactic Joust on my Roundabout. These three warriors, and perhaps a few others, will be your adversaries. In order to win, you must defeat each of them. Now, you must enter the Roundabout upon your mechanical beast, and I will explain the rules.' With no alternative, you obey. Turn to **48**.

22

Test your Luck. If you are Lucky, turn to **231**; if you are Unlucky, turn to **366**.

23

Dodging the enemy fire, you attack the gigantic Valioog mothership's single weak spot. Luckily, you are so close to the ship that it has trouble bringing many of its lasers to bear upon you.

STARFIRE
   VALIOOG   RATING 5   LASERS 4   SHIELDS 10

If you win, turn to **226**.

24

Your victory is short-lived, as the treacherous Marsatu knocks you down with a short club. 'Ha, ha!' he scoffs. 'You fight well for a "real", but you're so stupid!' He blows into an enormous whistle-ring encircling one of his fingers, and three more Prefectas appear. 'I have brought the spy along myself,' he informs them. 'Now, let's go and see L'Bastin!' The Prefectas seize you and take your weapons. Deduct 1 point from your SKILL. 'Yes,' they laugh. 'Let's visit L'Bastin.' They touch the obelisk, which wobbles aside, and you are dragged below, through a maze of corridors and halls. In one room Marsatu waves his arms. 'This was, until recently, the defence centre, crammed with complex computer systems. But my creator, L'Bastin the genius, decided that it would be safer to move the computers to another location. So you see, your mission was futile from the first!' Turn to 75.

25

After some time spent wandering about, you come upon a large, arched tunnel on your left and decide to follow it. Some distance along, you notice a black metal ring embedded in the ceiling. Will you step beneath the ring (turn to 2), or will you pass it to one side, and continue on your way (turn to 7)?

26

Smoke belches from a pipe in your craft. Several violent manoeuvres take place, and when the air finally clears, the Deik appears behind you. Your stinger slashes at his ship, but is blocked by a shield. Retaliating, the Deik extends a 'spiker'. You may:

Pull on a wire	Turn to 372
Touch a sensor disc	Turn to 176
Close your eyes and push, pull or kick any control you touch	Turn to 264

27

With a loud snap, the quill breaks off. Unluckily you have woken your guard, who scuttles over in a rage. 'So!' it cries, six claws on hips. 'Thought you'd escape, hey? Well, this'll keep you down!' Seizing a big stone, it knocks you unconscious. Your adventure is over.

28

During your furious foray with the robot, you smashed several large acid bottles whose contents dripped on to the floor. The acid has now eaten a hole in the metal plates, exposing two rooms and part of a passage below. These seem to provide the only ways to escape a hungry blob which has suddenly appeared at the doorway. But before you leave, you have time to look over and grab two of the following items.

>tibia bone
>robot's metal arm
>acid bottle
>jar with pickled brain
>grease-gun
>hypodermic syringe

When you have chosen two items, add them to your *Adventure Sheet*. Now, will you jump through the hole into the first room (turn to **274**), or the second room (turn to **124**), or into the passage (turn to **173**)?

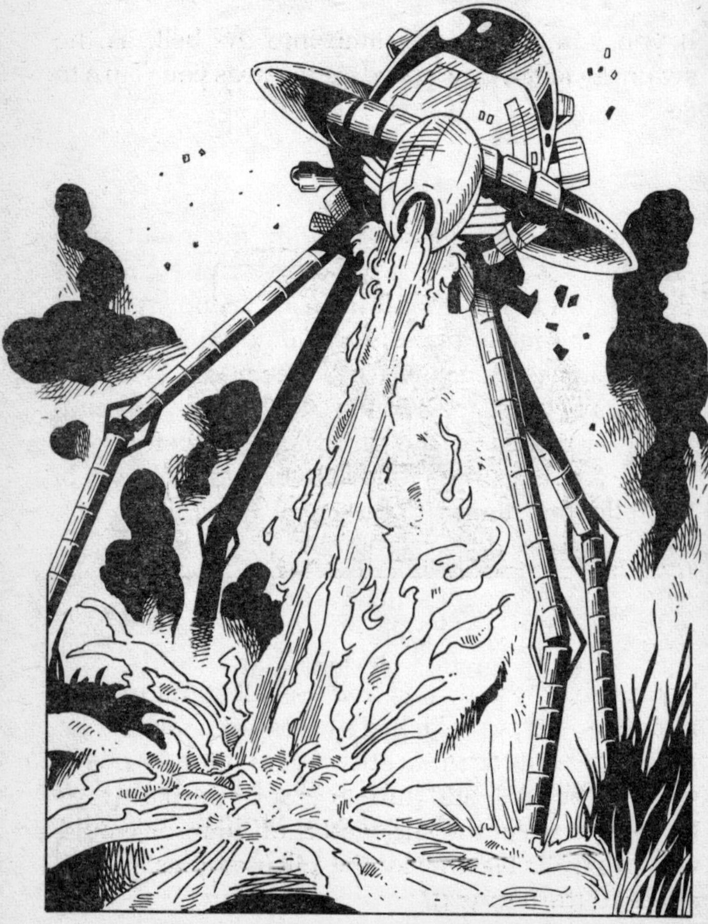

29

As you prepare to board the strange bell-ship, the spider-craft closes in. Using a flame-cannon, its rider engages you in a fearsome fire-fight.

PREFECTA   SKILL 8   STAMINA 8

If you win, you must climb into the bell, as the swamp-yacht is now speeding towards you. Turn to **80**.

30

You search the body and find a small titanium cube in his pouch; you take it. The creature stuck to the pillar now calls again to attract your attention. Will you use the red liquid (turn to **324**), or the blue (turn to **189**), to wash the sticky stuff off him, or would you prefer to blast away the pillar to which he is attached (turn to **373**)?

31

You follow a line of ragged starbrush along the base of a dune for several hundred yards, then run into a barrier: a sticky web. Savagely, you cut the web apart, but at this moment you are set upon by a many-eyed, eight-armed beast wielding rocks, clubs and knives.

AAROK SPIDER   SKILL 9   STAMINA 4

If you win, turn to **263**.

32

The enemy's barge eventually disappears from sight over the dunes, and you continue your journey in peace. Late in the day, only a few miles from the city, you come upon a tall metal structure. At first glance this resembles a peculiar, mushroom-shaped sculpture. Then you realize it is creaking; expanding out and up – it is alive! On a boulder near by squats an odd toad-faced creature, half your size. In a dignified voice, it speaks to you. 'Ah, sir, would you be so kind as to assist me? A precious heirloom of mine has been stolen by a scurrilous bandit – a human, in fact. He is locked in his dwelling yonder' pointing to the metal mushroom, 'and will not come out.' At some small inconvenience, you agree to aid the creature. Turn to **92**.

33

Suddenly there is a loud bang and a puff of smoke. 'Aargh!' screams Krill. 'Something's gone wrong!' He returns to you with his clothes singed and his moustache still smouldering. 'I'm afraid my plan misfired,' he reports. 'Your ship has been destroyed. Alas, there are no other spaceships, apart from Schaine's; to fly that you would need a Delphon flight-manual and hundreds of years' experience as a star-battleship's apprentice. Neither of these is available to you.' Stranded, your adventure is over.

34

You are attacked by a small, unmanned craft, launched from the *Grand Archipelago*'s main deck.

PIRATE
   DRONE   RATING 3   LASERS 6   SHIELDS 10

If you win, then your rapid manoeuvres against the drone have placed you on a new attack angle to your target. Turn to **107**.

35

Although you manage to zap one of the Brutes, the other, obviously Kogo's chef, strikes at you with a meat cleaver.

KOGO'S CHEF   SKILL 6   STAMINA 8

If you win, turn to **221**.

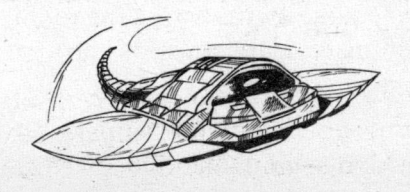

36

The Deik is unimpressed by your arrogant ripostes, and orders several heavies to teach you a lesson in good manners! Two gigantic Hulks jump over the bar and lumber towards you, broken bottles in hand.

	SKILL	STAMINA
BIG HULK	7	10
EVEN BIGGER HULK	5	14

Even if you win, you have been momentarily stunned. Turn to **72**.

37

Your tactics prove disastrous, as the bell-craft fills with mud and sludge through the open hatches. Within a short time, you are smothered.

38

You lean over to examine the plate, but stumble on to it. You seem to be falling for an eternity. Your adventure is over.

39

Thick green smoke swirls across the room, through which the monster leaps towards you.

GREEN GIANT   SKILL 8   STAMINA 10

If you win, turn to **50**.

40

You re-enter the *Starspray* – to find an enormous, very angry, very hungry-looking blob awaiting you. Since you know that your own weapons are not effective against blobs, you may make use of any items you possess to defend yourself; using the table below, add up the points for any of the following items you have in your possession. Then remove those items from your *Adventure Sheet*, as they are devoured by the blob!

	POINTS
flare pistol	1
chain	1
compressed-air canister	2
wrist-watch	1
club	1
chewing gum	2
tibia bone	3
robot's metal arm	1
acid bottle	1
jar with pickled brain	1
grease-gun	1
hypodermic syringe	2
electrostatic inducer	2
flame torch	1
oxygen cylinder	2
laminex sheet	2
3-D pictoscope	1
viscous negator	1
chair	1
blancmange	1

carving knife	1
leg of mutton	2
teapot	1
cinnamon stick	3
snooker cue	1
dumb-bell	1
cricket bat	1
medicine ball	2
skipping rope	1
darts	1
pot plant	1
strawberries	2
shovel	1
weed-killer	1
broom	1
plastic hose	2
wrench	1
hammer	1
sonic screwdriver	1
fire extinguisher	2
multifacetous aciduator	1
ball-bearings	2
revolver	1
peak cap	1
poison	2
can of beer	2
axe	1
box of cigars	2

If, before using any items to attack the blob, you have *less than* 13 points in total, turn to **297**; otherwise, turn to **232**.

41

The Redneck slams into your starship's tail which, luckily, is still protected by shields. Prudently you decide to exit light-warp prematurely, to examine the damage, before continuing. Back in 'real space', the damage appears to be slight: a few smouldering pods are quickly extinguished, and a blood-streak on the port retro easily removed. This time, you decide to continue in the less dangerous 4th-dimensional time-warp. However, before you can adjust your controls, you notice ahead of you a monstrous black hulk moving silently across the stars. Do you wish to enter the time-warp (turn to **164**), or examine the mysterious shape ahead (turn to **137**)?

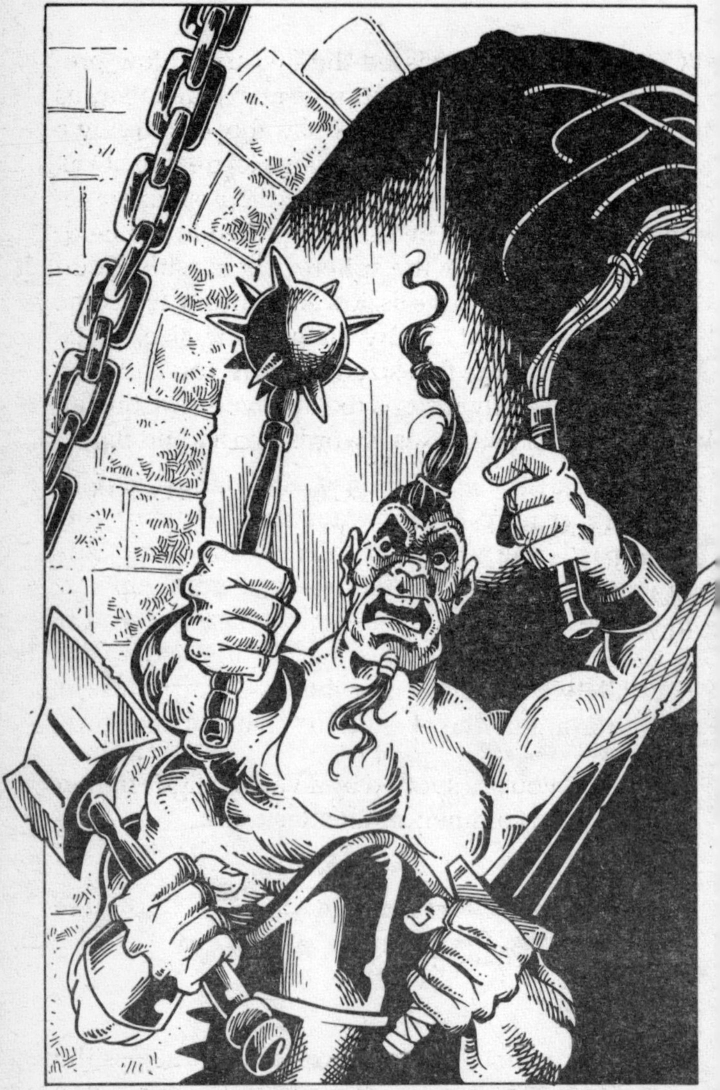

42

'Correct! You have passed the first trial. Now prepare for the second.' The strange man fades away as a massive arm appears in the sky above, carrying a mighty glass fortress. It is the same fortress the Deik was pawing earlier – although it did appear somewhat smaller then! The castle is placed in the field, and the arm departs the sphere. Then, with a loud rattle, the drawbridge is lowered and a fearsome multi-armed beast, many times your size, steps forth. Was this the flea-sized creature you had seen before? Haughtily it steps towards you, twirling an assortment of battleaxes, swords, maces and flails.

	SKILL	STAMINA
AXE ARM	10	2
SWORD ARM	8	4
MACE ARM	8	6
FLAIL ARM	6	8

If you win, turn to **201**.

43

Unluckily, you are spotted by a Valioog light-fighter captain, who commences an attack run.

LIGHT-
 FIGHTER   RATING 6   LASERS 2   SHIELDS 8

If you win, turn to **23**.

44

You brace yourself as the *Starspray* skips across the water, somersaults and, with a heavy splash, sinks to the bottom of the lake. Deduct 3 points from your STAMINA. With precious little time, you abandon the cabin and, exiting through an escape hatch, swim to the surface. A trail of foam and a few bubbles are all that remain to mark the grave-site of your spacecraft; by the time you have swum to shore, even these paltry signs have vanished. It seems that your adventure has already ended in disaster. Turn to **117**.

45

Reduce your oxygen supply by 3 points, and deduct 1 point from your STAMINA. Farkin, anticipating your blow, springs forward and head-butts you. Bursting for air, will you:

Try a strangle-hold?	Turn to **180**
Elbow his stomach?	Turn to **120**
Try a waist-clinch?	Turn to **95**

46

You break open the sphere and push two of your hands into the heavy steel power-gauntlets. Then, intending to grip the sides of the dome and clamber down to the entrance, you activate them. One of the gloves is faulty, however; it immediately curls itself into a useless, clenched fist, from which you cannot withdraw your hand. Furthermore, the switch is broken, so that the glove's power cannot be turned off! You will require a laser-saw to cut the gauntlet away – but meanwhile you have the use of three hands only. Deduct 1 point from your SKILL.

However, using the other glove, you still manage to wriggle down the dome's side towards the entrance. Marsatu is waiting for you. Turn to **363**.

47

There is a small explosion beneath your sphere, and your stinger slashes wildly through the water. As you sink towards the lake-bottom, the Deik's grabber rips the key from your hull, and he releases himself. A moment later, your lungs fill with water. That's your lot!

48

For this game, refer to *diagram 2* on the inside front cover. You enter the central (white) platform of the Roundabout. On the outermost (red) circle stand your three adversaries (in the positions shown in the diagram). 'Now,' announces the giant, 'the rules are simple. You are on a white circular platform from which you must *not* move. Before you are three rings: red, blue and yellow, each divided into twelve segments. Built upon some of these segments are screens (shown in black). The screens are high and you cannot see over them. It is possible at times for either yourself or your opponents to rotate the coloured rings, with their screens, in a manner which I will now describe . . .'

1. The game is conducted in *moves*, each of which consists of four *phases*.

2. During phase 1, you control the red ring; you must rotate it (and your opponents on it) either

one segment clockwise or two segments anti-clockwise. Your phase then ends.

3. During phase 2, Glip controls the red ring; he must rotate it one segment clockwise or one segment anti-clockwise. After doing so, he will check his position: if he has an unobstructed (screen-free) line of sight to you, he will charge across the rings and attack. If, however, his path is blocked by a screen, his phase ends.

4. During phase 3, Scuttlebug controls the blue ring; he must rotate it either one segment clockwise or not at all. Again, if after doing so he has an unobstructed view, he will attack. Otherwise his phase ends.

5. During phase 4, Mutant controls the yellow ring; he must rotate it one segment anti-clockwise. If after doing so he has an unobstructed view, he will attack; otherwise, his phase ends.

6. If you destroy an enemy, another warrior will appear on the red ring, in the same position as that just vacated.

7. The game ends victoriously for you only if you destroy at least one of each *type* of enemy. If you have not destroyed at least one of each type at the end of a move, you must begin the next move from step 2, above. However, you have a *maximum of four moves* to complete the game; otherwise, you will automatically be obliterated.

Giant Jym Ego drops a spotted handkerchief. 'Let

the game begin!' It is your phase first. If you have the ionic sphere, turn to **199**; otherwise, turn to **345**.

49

'Ha!' says Bric to Brac. 'What did I tell you?' Turn to **59**.

50

The gas finally clears. You take the titanium cube (the only item of interest you can readily pocket), and press a stud on the chair to raise the gate, as there are no other exits from the room. Next, you listen for any sounds before climbing out. But unluckily you are jumped on by the two Brutes, who had been waiting silently. The man in the white suit and his cat are standing near by, watching the fun! Turn to **287**.

51

The Deik's shell now springs wide open, revealing the clammy creature: a large, purple blotch. Contorting itself like dough, the Deik extends an ugly face with many eyes and nostrils, one large pointed ear, and several beaky mouths. A rubbery arm also appears and twines itself around a nearby curio: a small glass fortress imprisoning a flea-sized beast. The Deik eyes you suspiciously before squawking at you. 'Look, lads, seems like tonight's contestant is a volunteer! Ha, ha! Tell me: if you win, what will you claim as your prize? Come now, don't be bashful! You may choose anything from my collection!' Somewhat benumbed, you reply in a weak voice that what you would like is the Bulb-headed Bicephalon's brain. 'Ha!' cries the Deik. 'I should have guessed old Zud would send another one for it. Thought you'd steal it from right under my noses, eh? Well, I'll give it to ya' – if you're victorious. Take him to the Sphere of Three Trials!' A heavy-pawed Ogre-oid drags you to the floating orange sphere. 'Every night for over an 'undred years contestants 'ave gone into this 'ere ball,' it sneers, 'and ev'ry one of 'em's been done over. Not returned, like. Not only that, but none of 'em's ever got past the second trial neither! Ha! Don't fancy bein' in your shoes!' With a shove, the brute pushes you through the sphere's thin membrane, which re-seals around you. You are trapped! Turn to **351**.

52

You pilot the *Starspray* northwards towards Aarok's main spaceport at Central City. The city soon appears: a large blue-walled fortress shimmering in the dawn light. But suddenly a red beam streams out from one of the city towers, scoring a direct hit on your craft. Your port thruster is pierced. Although it does not explode, you will have to crash-land somewhere short of the spaceport. Will you veer towards a black swamp in the north-west (turn to **154**), or towards a purple desert in the north-east (turn to **84**)?

53

You take the Ixian's laser-rifle. Add 1 point to your SKILL. Now you may try to open the hatch by turning the handles in any combination you have not yet tried – either:

Turn the red handle clockwise, blue anti-clockwise	Turn to 386
Turn red and blue anti-clockwise	Turn to 118
Turn red anti-clockwise, blue clockwise	Turn to 192

54

You awaken with blurred eyes and a terrible headache. Deduct 1 point from your STAMINA. You are alone and so, after a short wait, you go in search of your hosts. Leaving the parlour, will you follow the passage left (turn to 326), or right (turn to 284)?

55

You are confronted by a gruesome, twisted monster with a long green head and clawed arms extending from its cheeks. Smashing the window-shutters, it seizes you and flings you, head first, into its gaping mouth. Your adventure is over.

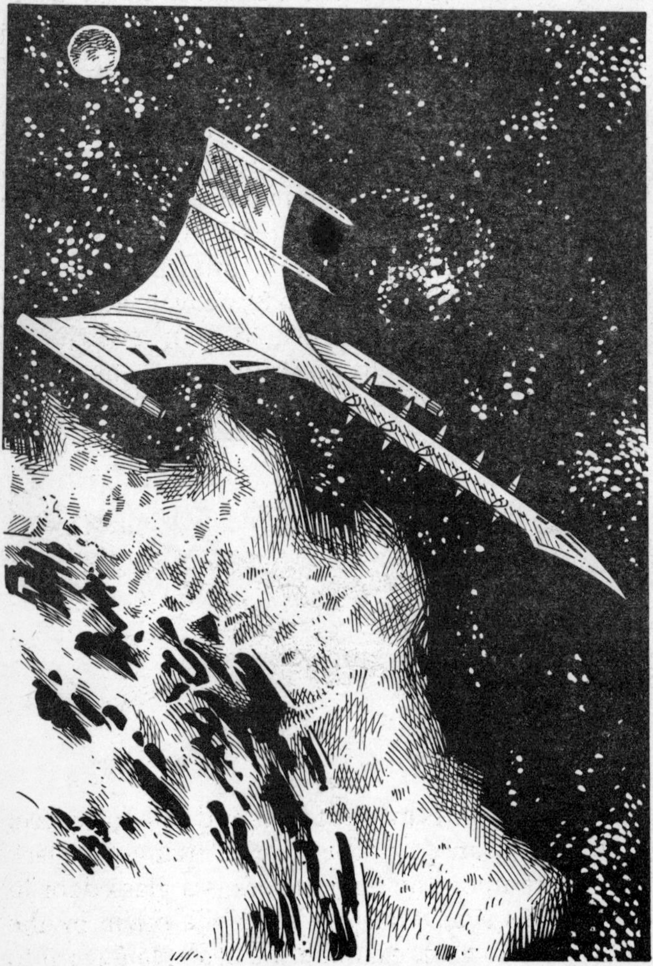

56

With a judder, you re-enter 'real space' in the Calibrowi solar system: a sub-system of fifteen planets inhabited by millions of life-forms. Not far away resides the heart of the system: the ruby-red dwarf-star, Calibrow. But now the sun appears pale and faltering: the Valioog ship is already plundering its energy . . . Within a few moments, you locate the ship: a long, thin vessel, just to the right of the sun. Will you switch your craft into a computer-controlled attack run (turn to **8**); activate additional anti-detector shields (turn to **70**); switch off thrusters and glide into attack range (turn to **121**); or attempt a computer-scan of your enemy (turn to **163**)?

57

The tetrahedron is made of glass and is about six feet high: it is floating, a foot above a triangular black base-plate upon the floor. There is a glass door in the prism's side. You may enter the prism by the door (turn to **224**), examine the base plate (turn to **38**) or, if you haven't done so already, approach the distant manor-house (turn to **142**).

58

Glip now turns the red ring one segment clockwise, creating a free path to you. Brandishing his electro-lance, he charges on his armoured steed into your flanks. You are unable to bring all your laser-cannon to bear on him in time.

	RATING	LASERS	SHIELDS
GLIP	4	3	8
GRASSHOPPER	–	3	10

If you win, another Glip appears on the vacated spot on the red ring. Scuttlebug this time decides not to rotate the blue ring, but still he cannot attack. Finally, Mutant rotates the yellow ring one segment anti-clockwise to end his phase. The fourth and final move begins. You still need to destroy a Scuttlebug to win. Will you rotate the red ring one segment clockwise (turn to 310), or two segments anti-clockwise (turn to 361)?

59

'Wrong!' replies Bric, and blasts you to atoms.

60

At the end of a passage, you enter a small, cuboid room which obviously serves as the space station's laboratory. Upon wire racks in the centre of the room lie a pile of bones, while to one side stands a spindly, silver robot. 'Gotcha!' it grates as it grabs you with three multi-purpose arms. 'I'm this star-station's automated pathologist. Let's see what makes *you* tick!' With unnerving strength, the robot hurls you on to a wire rack and swivels one of its tinsnip claws towards your throat. You must defend yourself!

ROBOT
  PATHOLOGIST   SKILL 8   STAMINA 8

If you win, turn to **28**.

61

You take a sip. Ugh! It is putrid. Your hosts burst into fits of laughter. 'No, no,' Marsatu says at last, 'that is *foot* ointment!' Now understanding, you remove your boots and place your feet in the soothing liquid. Marsatu does likewise with the green liquid, while Bok serves you both a tankard of hot, spicy mead which tastes delightful. After refilling and draining your mug several more times, you roll to the floor, beaming a foolish grin. With paralysis creeping on, you close your eyes and drift into a jolly dream, while the night outside passes slowly and quietly. Turn to **54**.

62

You re-enter 'real space' and examine your spaceship. The fungus has grown to enormous size, covering most of the starboard thruster and part of the fuselage. It has also changed to a light blue colour. You may decide to leave the ship and cut it off (turn to **244**), or search for a planet and, passing through its atmosphere, burn it off (turn to **213**).

63

You hear the Prefectas enter the laboratory. After a casual search, they depart in the direction of the air-tube, and Vault 6. You decide to stay put and rest for a while. Fifteen minutes later, you notice a chemical sludge entering the bench through a side-port, forming a pool around you. It is slightly acidic and burns your skin. Deduct 2 points from your STAMINA. You now realize that you are in one of the tubs used to manufacture Prefectas. But the mixture in your vat will never form properly . . . A while later, you hear the newly congealed, over-salted Prefectas struggling from the other tubs. They are arguing among themselves even as they leave the laboratory, going in the direction of the air-tube. It seems that the fun is about to begin! Turn to **187**.

64

A heavy, grinning robot appears, then exits through a large hatch. But at this moment, the bell-craft is struck by an electrical charge. Circuits fizzle and spark, and the hatch is jammed wide open, allowing two Prefectas, in combat uniforms, to storm the ship. You must fight!

	SKILL	STAMINA
PREFECTA SERGEANT	8	10
PREFECTA TROOPER	8	8

If you win, will you steer eastwards, while deploying starmines (turn to **198**), submerge into the swamp (turn to **37**), or order the computer to implement action plan number 358 (turn to **358**)?

65

The old man squeals angrily. Turn to **384**.

66

From the cube issues a puff of smoke. Its odour is making you queasy. During the following combat, deduct 1 point from your SKILL temporarily for the duration of this battle. Turn to **39**.

67

You reach for your laser-pistol, but giant Jym Ego is too quick. He punches you with his mallet-like fist and sends you sprawling. Deduct 3 points from your STAMINA. If you are still alive, you pocket your dislodged front teeth and stagger to your feet. Turn to **21**.

68

Quickly you cut a spindly root from the tree and form it into a crude lasso. When the spider-craft is within range, you snare it; it topples forward into the mud. Unfortunately it also falls on *you*! You are squashed in an instant.

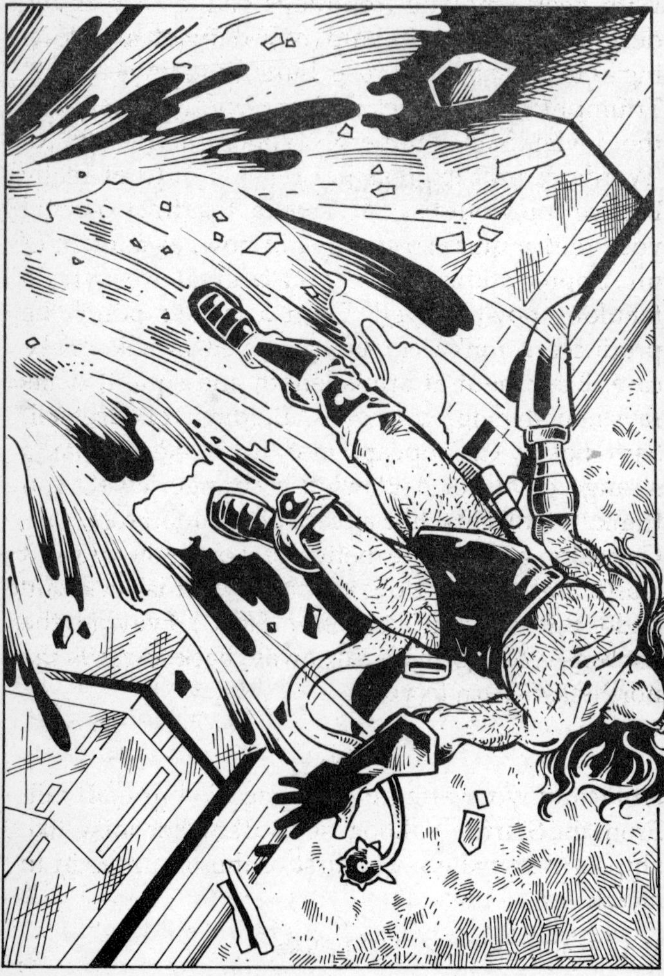

69

With heels smoking, the Mogs bounds across the deck, into the lake. Its ship, now defunct and glowing a curious shade of rose, bursts into tiny embers. Triumph! Steering back to shore, you are greeted by the jovial Sam. 'Superb! Wonderful!' he cries. 'Words cannot express my relief. I did not really believe you would . . . er, I mean, I hadn't expected your return quite so soon. And now, as a token of my appreciation, I give you a great treasure: a fabulous power-jewel!' From a leather pouch he produces a milky crystal, wrapped in silk. 'Take care! Examine it at arm's length and squint, or its rays may damage your eyes.' Bidding you farewell, Sam hastily disappears into the reeds. What a strange creature! And what a strange jewel, you think. It looks just like a piece of common rock-salt. Curiosity getting the better of you, you draw it closer and closer. Now you taste it. It is rock-salt! (Add this to your *Adventure Sheet*.) Leaving the gardens, you storm angrily away, back towards the north-east. Turn to **318**.

70

Unluckily, your attempts to conceal your craft fail. From the Starfire Valioog, several smaller spike-like ships are launched. The first of these buzzes in to attack you.

VALIOOG STARFIGHTER
                  RATING 5   LASERS 4   SHIELDS 10

If you win, will you scan the starfighter debris for

valuables, (turn to **260**); dart towards the Valioog mothership at Mach 6 (turn to **369**); operate a computer-scan, if you have not done so already (turn to **163**); or perform an 'Eigenvector roll', to attack another starfighter from the rear (turn to **320**)?

71

With a whoosh of escaping gas, you attach the *Starspray* to a circular, concertina air-corridor and, donning a space helmet, prepare to enter the space station. Ahead of you, at the extreme end of the air-tube, is a translucent, semi-ovoid air-lock which begins to rotate slowly as you approach. Will you enter the air-lock when it is in a horizontal position (turn to **382**), or a vertical position (turn to **209**)?

72

Test your Luck. If you are Lucky, turn to **251**; if you are Unlucky, turn to **139**.

73

All square-shaped tiles change colour again: orange to green, green to blue, blue to orange. Will you step on tile E1 (turn to **68**), or tile D2 (turn to **3**)?

74

The door opens, and a long, wispy-grey thread shoots out at you. Your limbs tingle and you collapse to the floor. Deduct 3 points from your STAMINA. Just in time, you close the door on the thread, which wriggles and retracts. You decide to follow the passage. Turn to **161**.

75

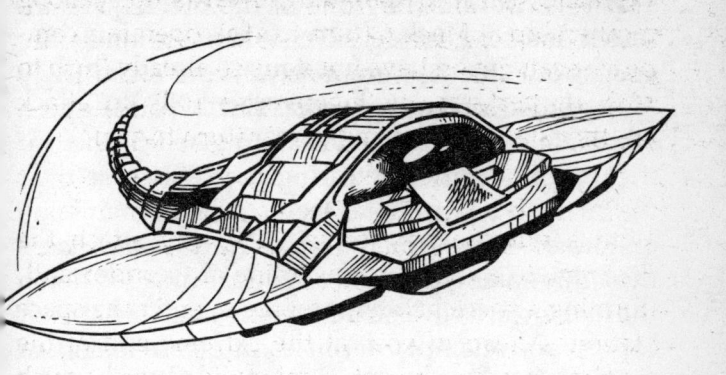

Eventually you enter a long, crystal chamber, at the end of which is a cylindrical tank, eight feet high and three feet wide, mounted on three rubber wheels. Curling from the tank's base is an enormous ivory horn; pricking into its sides are half a dozen shiny metal quills. With creeping dread, you recognize the bizarre contraption: it is a Crump's Posidon Tank, a diabolically efficient torture chamber manufactured by the Questions-and-Answers Division of the notorious family enterprise, Elmer Crump & Sons. Many varieties of posidon tank are in use throughout the multiverses, but the Mark IVP model, before you now, operates in the following fashion. The intended victim is bound and immersed upside down in the cylinder's oily liquid. He is able to breathe, speak or scream only through a rubber mouthpiece and hose, leading into the ivory horn. Within the oil exist six tiny mechanical creatures: Crump's patented tinselfish. Each tinselfish is controlled by one of the metal quills inserted into the tank's side. When the quills are almost out, the fish are inactive, and swim lazily around their victim, only occasionally pausing for a nibble; but when the quills are pushed further in, they become furious, tearing mercilessly at their victim with sharp metal teeth. Will your mission end here? Will you be the tank's next victim? These thoughts enter your mind as you are dragged down the hall towards it. You may wish to lash out at your captors and attempt a daring escape (turn to **159**), or will you desist struggling and, hopefully, find the means to escape later on (turn to **322**)?

76

The droid is grateful for your protection. 'But I know that you also are in need of aid,' it buzzes. 'Follow me, then, for I return to my master in the Jedburg Caves. He may be able to assist you.' Having no better plan, you follow the droid for many hours. Just before dawn, you espy before you a huge wall of rounded boulders; beneath the wall are hundreds of cave openings. The droid selects one of these and leads you inside. Turn to **319**.

77

Picking up a cue, you roll the white ball into the reds, splitting them and knocking a red into the top left-hand pocket. Next, you aim at an orange ball, intending to put it into the centre pocket. Orange ball? You realize that snooker does not use an orange ball. Cautiously, you touch the ball with the end of your cue, only to see it wobble about and wriggle up the stick: it is a baby orange blob! Now, from a corner pocket oozes its mother – a much larger blob. Breaking away from the table, you prepare a hasty departure from the hall, as the mother blob re-forms on the floor and comes rolling towards you. During your flight, however, you do have time to pick up any two of the following items, which may prove useful later on.

> snooker cue
> dumb-bell
> cricket bat
> medicine ball
> skipping rope
> darts

When you have chosen two items, add them to your *Adventure Sheet*. Now, will you flee on an exercise scooter (turn to 266), or slide down a transit pole (turn to 103)?

78

After remaining hidden for several hours, you leave the shaft and take an unoccupied tube-car to the city. You pass by many stations before disembarking. Turn to 323.

79

Try as you may, the cylinder will not budge. After a pause, Zud continues, 'Or, as I was saying, it might take Gnasha several days to break out. But I know that I wouldn't want that tube buried inside me when he escapes, no sir! No doubt you wouldn't like it either. Well, this is your lucky day! My generosity knows no bounds; I also have a key to remove the cylinder. I will offer you both keys you require in return for, er, a small task I would like you to perform for me.' Will you help Zud (turn to **270**), or do you prefer to throw the nearest flask of acid at him instead (turn to **102**)?

80

You climb into the strange bell and close the hatch. Its pilot now appears: a very old humanoid with green and grey striped skin, and leaning on a cane. Silently, he ushers you into a control cabin where, on a vidi-screen, you watch him fire a laser-cannon at the swamp-yacht. After a short mêlée, the yacht retreats, trailing a cloud of smoke, and the pilot returns to you. 'Heh, heh! Haven't had so much excitement in years! But allow me an introduction: I am Rhio, the caretaker.' Rhio is an Aarokian, one of the original inhabitants of the planet. He had been left behind, more than three hundred years ago, to look after the world until the radiation levels had reduced and the Aarokians could return. Unluckily the race was decimated by a space plague, and now only Rhio is left. 'But I'm not long for this world,' he continues. 'Soon I will die and our race will end . . .' Turn to **179**.

81

Epicurien the Torturer pounds his fist into your chest again. This time he notices the tube. 'What's this – valuable, I'll bet! Well, I'll relieve you of it this instant.' He pinches the cylinder's end with a pair of pliers and begins extracting it from your chest. Deduct 2 points from your STAMINA. Eventually, with a forceful tug, the cylinder comes loose, flies up into the air, and drops down again – plop! – straight into Epicurien's back. Of course, it immediately embeds itself in him. 'What devilish trick is this,' he screams at you. 'Aaargh! Aargh!' He turns a somersault in anger. You can hear Gnasha finally break his way out of the tube; Epicurien's end is mercifully swift. When Gnasha has finished its meal, it hops to the ground. 'Ah, titanium, my *favourite* meal!' it says. Wishing to take advantage of the situation, you say enticingly, 'Come over here, then. I've got some nice titanium chains I will allow you to partake of!' *Test your Luck*. If you are Lucky, turn to **330**: if you are Unlucky, turn to **181**.

82

Your lasers scorch the *Grand Archipelago*, but cause it only superficial damage.

Starspray: Pitch +54 ... Roll +32 ... Yaw +13 ...
Enemy: Pitch +35 ... Roll +60 ... Yaw +13 ...
Relative speed 2000 ...

Will you:

Maintain speed, pitch +62.5, roll −20, yaw 37.5?	Turn to **98**
Maintain speed, pitch +50, roll −50?	Turn to **177**
Halve speed, maintain course?	Turn to **366**

The inn is large, dingy and dirty, and so are its occupants, a wide variety of rogues and scoundrels from all over the galaxy. At a drinking-pit, a scar-faced, one-eyed Oc is fingering a silver knife and evilly viewing a gang of five-eyed Tuffits; by the wall a solitary Grey-hulker drains a keg-sized tankard, then devours the tankard and orders another; a couple of Jellimen wobble towards the bar – everyone steps out of *their* way; the room is filled with hyperactive pickpockets, and you must continually check your gear. This is no place for the squeamish! Upon the bar is a large, clam-shaped shell: it is the Deik himself. The shell is closed and appears to be asleep. Amidst the throng, the Deik's wondrous and wide-ranging display of antiques and curios is scattered – many of them having been bolted to the floor or set with alarms. A number of the objects are quite bizarre and they attract your attention: several good-sized tapestries; a large orange sphere hovering in mid-air; a heavy brass gong; a man-sized candle; and, of course, the crystal decanter containing the Bicephalon's preserved brain. You dare not approach too close to the decanter yet for fear of arousing suspicion – so will you move over to the brass gong (turn to **214**), or the candle (turn to **365**), or turn towards the drinking-pits instead (turn to **301**)?

84

You brace yourself as the *Starspray* skims over a dune crest and plummets into a valley of sand and ash. Deduct 2 points from your STAMINA. After a brief reconnaissance, you gather your equipment and depart on foot towards the distant city. Turn to **376**.

85

You grapple with the demented man, but he dies in your arms. Now, locking the drone to your own ship, you prepare to leave. First, however, you may go through the belongings of the deceased. You may choose any two items from the following list.

> revolver
> peak cap
> poison
> can of beer
> axe
> box of cigars

When you have chosen two items, add them to your *Adventure Sheet*, then turn to **40**.

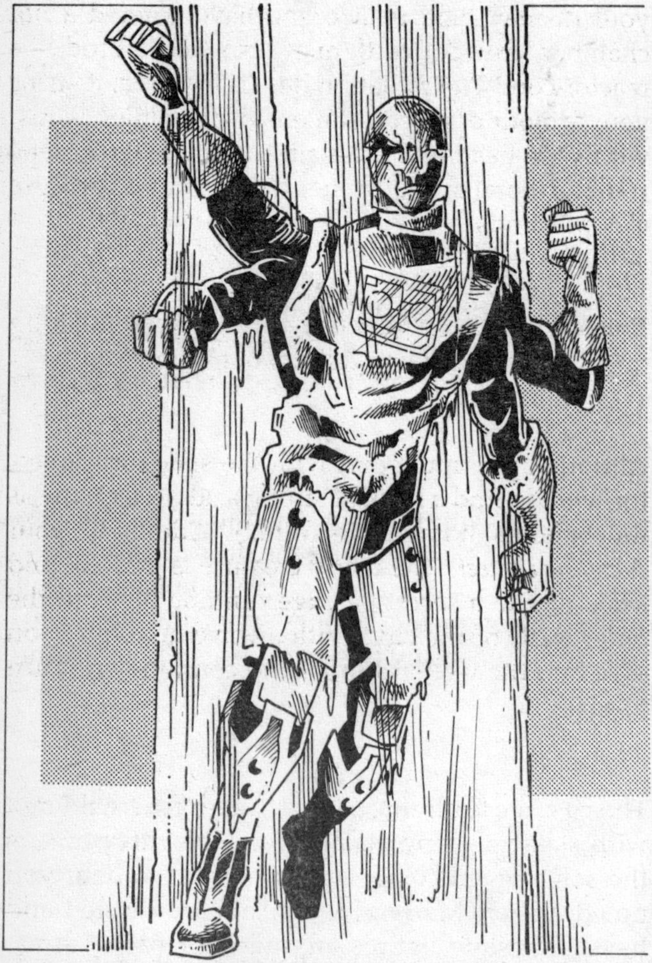

86

You follow the pillar down into the next level. To your dismay, you realize you have entered a hot chamber, crowded with many more cobalt rods – a reactor core! The radiation here is extreme; it strips your armour of its pan-dimensional abilities. Thus, with your head and arms protruding from a metal rod and bombarded by neutrons, your adventure abruptly ends.

87

Roll one die. If you roll 1 or 2, turn to **335**; if you roll 3 or 4, turn to **352**; if you roll 5 or 6, turn to **64**.

88

Although you must part with the spectron projector, you do find a flask of strong acid (in fact, this is the bandit's homemade drink!). Add it to your *Adventure Sheet*. The toady creature is grateful and leads you to a secret passage running beneath the outer walls of the city. With a wave goodbye, you dive into the well-lit tunnel and continue on. Turn to **323**.

89

The passage leads into a large, rough cavern littered with stalactites and stalagmites. The entire area is the same green colour as the horrible vapour you noted earlier. Many of the pillars are twisted and have grotesque figures around their bases: arms, legs, tentacles, claws and wings all protrude. Obviously they were once real creatures which have been covered with a sticky green substance that drips from the roof. Near one pillar, you hear a moan. Investigating, you find a hairy, bulb-eyed thing chained against the pillar. The sticky stuff covers most of his face. 'Help me, before it's too late,' he pleads. 'There are pits in the floor filled with liquid. Use it to wash this off me, please!' There are indeed pits in the floor: some filled with red liquid, and some with blue liquid. Just as you are on the point of asking the creature which you should use, a white-haired old man creeps up behind you, and gives you a push with his staff. *Test your Luck*. If you are Lucky, turn to **308**; if you are Unlucky, turn to **256**.

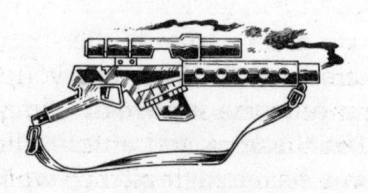

90

The polarizer malfunctions; an ominous burst of red light streams from the device and runs through your entire craft. Your adventure is over, as you receive an instantaneous, lethal radiation dose.

91

Krill returns. 'Follow me, your spacecraft is at the cave's entrance.' The sight of your ship, looking as good as new, delights you. Krill chuckles, 'I put it through a time-loop, so that it never crashed; in fact, it was never even struck by a lightning bolt! Now, perhaps you will do me one courtesy before you leave.' He explains that his people plan to attack the Delphon craft in the evening, and that you could help them greatly. 'The interferometer will immobilize their ship for only a short time. If we do not destroy them quickly, then they will try to take off, in order to bring all their guns to bear on us. If this happens, we would need you or someone like you to make an attack on them in your spacecraft and force them down again.' You agree, and Krill gives you an ear-twinge: a small, conical device which clips on to your earlobe. 'Wait here in your spacecraft, and attack when I give you the appropriate signal.' Turn to 313.

92

The toady creature points out to you the heavily barred entrance to the strange dwelling. In a short time, you cut the bars and enter a dim passage. Suddenly, you hear a high-pitched whine from the darkness ahead. Will you kneel down and draw your laser-pistol (turn to 183), or brace yourself, ready to throw your electro-javelin (turn to 220)?

93

As you turn the handles, a metal panel in the passage slides open, and a heavily armed creature springs from the niche. It is short, stubby and roughly humanoid, except that it has no head or neck: an Ixian! Three colourful bulbous eyes, mounted on its chest, glare at you as it mocks, 'Can't read signs, eh? Well, danger is what you've found.

Time to die, four-arms!' A light-bolt sizzles past your head as you dive to the floor, drawing your pistol.

IXIAN   SKILL 9   STAMINA 6

If you win, turn to 53.

94

You exit the room and run down the passage, with Zud in close pursuit. Peculiarly, his machine is jumping and jerking crazily, not entirely obeying his commands. Obviously, you must have injured the Bicephalon's brain when you stepped on it. But the machine still manages to catch up with you. Too late, you turn to fight it, as a heavy pan-headed weapon swats you against a wall. Your adventure is over.

95

Suddenly Farkin whirls around and flips you over his shoulder. Crashing to the ground, you are helpless as the gangster rips your chest open with his powerful clawed legs. Your adventure is over.

96

With a wrenching screech and a splitting of stones, the *Starspray* falls heavily on the shingles. Its nose-cone digs deep into the bank, the ship cartwheels and, with a smack, comes to rest beside a large tree. Deduct 4 points from your STAMINA. Even worse is to come: you stagger from the escape hatch only just in time, as the tree, angered by the appearance of your craft, seizes it with an enormous gnarled root, and hurls it far out into the lake. It seems that your adventure has already ended in disaster. Turn to **117**.

97

Hastily, you wrap your wounds within the soothing leaves. The 'oint' performs properly, and you recover all the STAMINA points you just lost due to the burns. Dr Strangething, still up on the clock tower, now calls to attract your attention. Turn to **221**.

98

Your craft is burned by an acid spray. Reduce your SHIELDS by 1 point *permanently*.

Starspray: Pitch +9 . . . Roll +82 . . . Yaw −18 . . .
Enemy: Pitch 35 . . . Roll +60 . . . Yaw +13 . . .
Relative speed 2000 . . .

Will you:

Maintain speed, pitch +5, yaw −13?	Turn to **269**
Maintain speed, pitch −10, roll +60, yaw −18?	Turn to **336**
Halve speed, pitch −15, yaw −13?	Turn to **366**

99

Now, all circle-shaped tiles change colour: orange to green, green to blue, blue to orange. No square tiles change colour. Next, will you step on tile A1 (turn to **273**), or tile B2 (turn to **309**)?

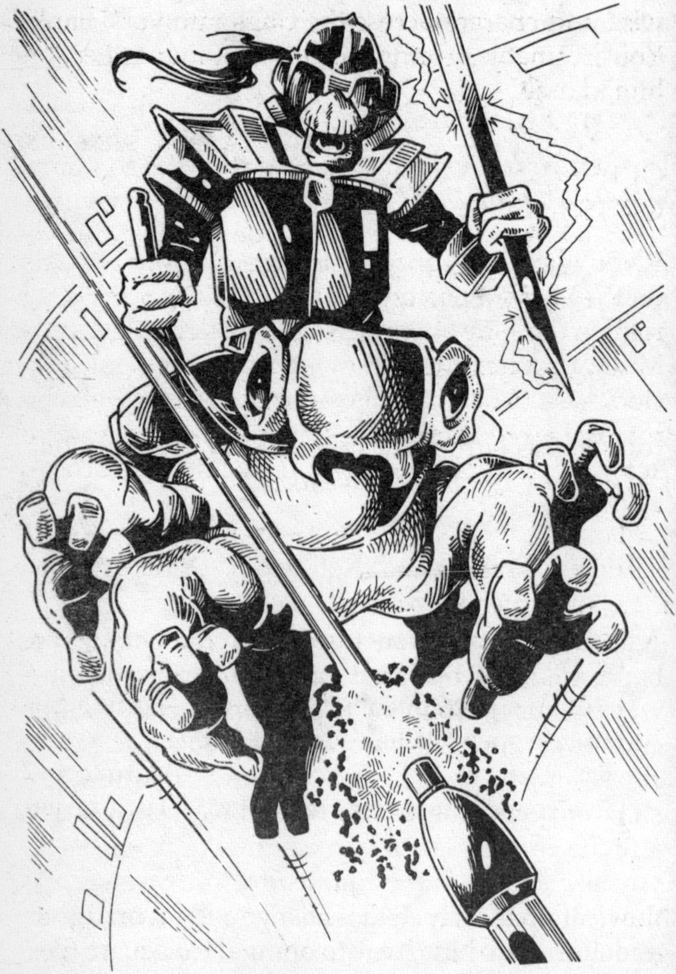

100

The new Glip turns the red ring one segment clockwise and charges across the rings into your flank. You are unable to bring your laser-cannon to bear on him in time.

	RATING	LASERS	SHIELDS
GLIP	4	3	8
GRASSHOPPER	–	3	10

If you win, then, once again, another Glip appears on the vacated position on the red ring. Scuttlebug rotates the blue ring one segment clockwise, then Mutant rotates the yellow ring one segment anti-clockwise. The third move ends. Next, will you rotate the red ring one segment clockwise (turn to 106), or two segments anti-clockwise (turn to 299)?

101

As you head away from the wharf, your engines are badly damaged by a heat-gun, firing from the tube-way building. Wobbling precariously, you steer the craft over the high blue wall of Central City and crash-land in an overgrown park. Enemy scout-ships appear in the sky above, and you leap towards a flight of steps leading to a subway station. Here you take an old underground monorail carriage into the heart of the city. Eventually you abandon the car and head off along a broad, triangular passage. Turn to 323.

102

A direct hit results, and Zud melts in an instant. Unfortunately, try as you may, the cylinder will not budge. Deduct 1 point from your STAMINA through exhaustion. Recklessly, you search the room for a key. You find hundreds of them – although none seems to fit the cylinder's lock. Dejectedly, you depart, to continue your mission, believing that nothing can save you from an evil fate. Turn to **7**.

103

You proceed via several passages and air-elevators, until you reach a drone launch-away tube. Within it is a spherical, iron-clad drone, suitable for carrying out minor repairs on the station. You enter the drone and lock its hatch; then, placing the craft on manual control, you launch yourself into space, gradually manoeuvring towards the *Starspray*. Suddenly, you are distracted by a moan coming from behind the drone's console. Then a bony-faced man appears, only half conscious. 'Heh, heh!' he coughs at you. 'You, I bet you're a blob, aren't you? You nasty great jellybean! Well, I may be the last of the crew, but you can eat me, too – if you care to die: I've poisoned m'self!' He swings an old revolver in your direction. You must defend yourself.

LUDO KLUDWIG   SKILL 7   STAMINA 4

If you win, turn to **85**.

104

Pulling out this book activates an electronic trigger, which sets one of the knick-knacks into motion. It is a multi-eyed security robot. It whirls towards you, blurting out a message, 'Intruder alert! Intruder alert! Shoot first, question later!'

SECURITY ROBOT   SKILL 9   STAMINA 4

If you win, you may remove a book which you had not previously examined:

Poets of the 57th Century	Turn to **355**
Baba's Book of Homemade Wines	Turn to **305**

105

Reduce your oxygen supply by 2 points. Your chop stuns Farkin, but he maintains his smothering hold. Will you:

Neck-chop again?	Turn to **45**
Try a bear-hug?	Turn to **207**
Knee-kick Fog Farkin?	Turn to **120**

106

The Glip turns the red ring one segment anti-clockwise, and charges along a clear path into your flank.

	RATING	LASERS	SHIELDS
GLIP	4	3	8
GRASSHOPPER	–	3	10

If you win, a new Glip appears on the vacated spot

on the red ring. Next, it is Scuttlebug's phase. He decides not to rotate the blue ring. Turn to **212**.

107

Your ship is gunned by a frost-ray. Reduce your SHIELDS by 1 point *permanently*. Your screen now suggests:

Starspray: Pitch +19 ... Roll +82 ... Yaw −8 ...
Enemy: Pitch +35 ... Roll +60 ... Yaw +13 ...
Relative speed 1000 ...

Will you:

Accelerate to 2000, yaw 3.5?	Turn to **148**
Maintain speed, roll 105, yaw 5?	Turn to **203**
Maintain speed, pitch 20, yaw 5?	Turn to **399**

108

Outside is a beautiful blonde Delphon sprite, wearing a dress of gold, crystals and glass. Her eyes flash towards you, paralysing you in the doorway. Her hands grasp a chain, restraining two horrible beasts with long green heads, mouths in their foreheads, and clawed arms extending from their cheeks and thighs. The monsters are drooling and snarling at you, but the sprite quietens them. 'Hush, my beauties!' she whispers. 'Your bellies are full of manflesh already. I've a better use for this one.' With that, she approaches and touches you lightly on the temples with her forefinger, then on your cheeks and thighs. 'I am Schaine the sprite,' she says. 'I see you are a sceptic, you do not trust to the power of magic. Well, soon now, you will.' Laughing, Schaine turns and leads her beasts away into the gloom. Your paralysis begins to wear off, and you return, stiff-legged, to the confines of the hut. In the morning you feel a little uneasy, as lumpy nodules have appeared on your cheeks and thighs, and your forehead is cracked and bleeding. Do you wish to leave the village via Spitflak's Street (turn to **160**), or further investigate the buildings during daylight (turn to **380**)?

109

Your shield lowers and you are struck by a great mattock: your sphere cracks and flounders. Sinking below the Deik's craft, you can clearly see the key attached beneath. In a final attempt to retrieve it, will you:

Kick a foot lever?	Turn to **47**
Punch your ship's control panel?	Turn to **338**

110

You made it! You step off the tiles, which revert to their original colour pattern, and Dr Strangething follows your path across. Then you both enter the glass prism and are whisked away to the surface and find yourselves close to the manor-house. Dr Strangething now points a tentacle at the clock tower's face. 'There is the cursor,' he says, 'disguised as one of the clock hands. Ingenious, yes?' The tower is smooth, black granite, but the doctor, employing the suckers on his three tentacle-legs, begins to climb, while you stand guard at its base. After perhaps a quarter of an hour, the doctor reaches the clock-face, and begins to prise one of the hands loose. At this moment, two Brutes suddenly appear around a corner. You may dive to the ground and laser them (turn to 35), leap at them with your laser-sword on maximum power (turn to 127), or, if you have any, hurl a flask of acid at them (turn to 18).

111

Brac chortles, as Bric shakes his face ruefully. Turn to 59.

112

Your cabin flashes with the sparks of a delta-ray. Deduct 2 points from your STAMINA.

Starspray: Pitch +21.5 . . . Roll +112 . . .
  Yaw +19.5 . . .
Enemy: Pitch +35 . . . Roll +60 . . .
  Yaw +13 . . .
Relative speed 1000 . . .

You may:

Maintain speed and course	Turn to **22**
Maintain speed, pitch +2.5, roll +90, yaw +37.5	Turn to **135**
Halve speed, pitch +30, roll +5	Turn to **347**

113

Standing in the space-ball rink, you hurl the egg-shaped ball hard against a wall, from which it rebounds with increased velocity. The ball bounces at obscure angles; at times you must dodge and flip clear of its path. You survive for one minute and twenty seconds in the rink, before the fast ball becomes too dangerous; so you decide to step outside. During the time you were in play you were hit only twice: deduct 2 points from your STAMINA. The result of your game is a score of sixty points (eighty seconds equals eighty points, less two glancing blows of ten points each). Sixty points would put you just outside the 'professional' category: a good result indeed. Now, will you turn your hand to snooker (turn to **77**), or exit the gymnasium via a sloping glide-away passage (turn to **103**)?

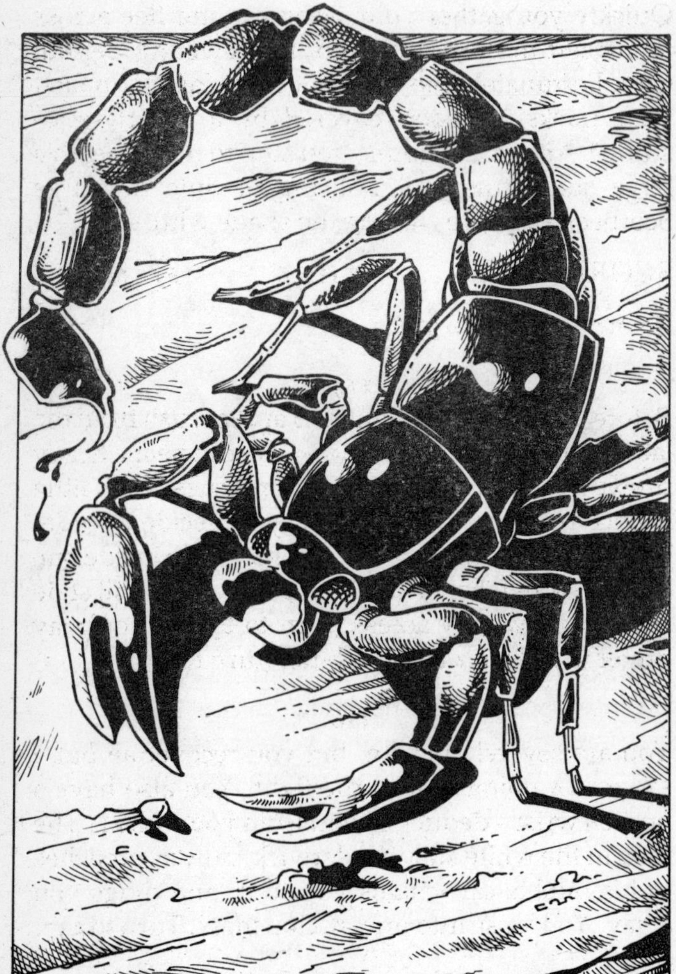

114

Quickly you gather your weapons and flee across the desert in the direction of the towering Central City. Fortunately the spiders do not follow (in fact, your tracks are soon covered by a desert sandstorm). After a few hours, you stop to rest beneath a large sun-cactus, not noticing in time the large Scorbeetle you are sharing the shade with.

SCORBEETLE   SKILL 6   STAMINA 8

If you win, turn to **377**.

115

Before you can stop them, the Yappies rush from the laboratory and raise the alarm. You can hear a heavy thud as a squad of Prefectas approaches. With little chance of defending yourself, you decide to hide. There are two alternatives: you may hide inside one of the wooden benches, the tops of which will slide back to allow easy access (turn to **63**), or you may prefer to hide in a metal cabinet (turn to **13**).

116

You are severely beaten, but you recover all but 2 STAMINA points lost in the fight. You also have a broken wrist – deduct 1 point from your SKILL. The man in the white suit, Woderwick, now approaches in his bubble-car, chains you to it, and drags you away. You lapse into unconsciousness. Turn to **237**.

117

For a while you sit disconsolately upon the bank, pondering your fate. Then, unexpectedly, you observe, wading from the lake, the three-faced droid you had scooped up earlier. It is carrying the high-tech device you could not make sense of. The droid passes into some trees, the rim of a broad forest, and is lost to view. You may wish to follow the droid (turn to **261**), or swim out to your ship to salvage some of its contents (turn to **302**); or you may decide to set off up the vale, hoping to find a village and obtain help (turn to **344**).

118

Disconcertingly, a small hatch in the ceiling clicks open, revealing two lamps: one red and one blue. These focus a purple heat-beam on you, shrivelling your skin as you beat a hasty retreat back along the tunnel. Deduct 2 points from your STAMINA. You decide to look for an easier entrance to Vault 2. Turn to **238**.

119

At the door, you trip over and accidentally put your foot right through the Bicephalon's brain, before departing with it. Although several critters chase you, you easily outdistance them, and return to Zud's chambers. Turn to **129**.

120

Reduce your oxygen supply by 2 points. Farkin topples to the ground, with you falling on top. Now, at some advantage, will you:

Try a head-lock? Turn to **268**

| Try to punch him in the eye? | Turn to 95 |
| Hit him with the pommel of your laser-sword? | Turn to 357 |

121

From the Valioog's portals, a cluster of vacuum-bomb torpedoes are launched. *Test your Luck*. If you are Lucky, turn to 342; if you are Unlucky, turn to 389.

122

Quickly you cut a spindly root from the tree and make a crude lasso from it. When the scooter is within range, you snare it, sending it spinning into the mud. But its riders, two quick-witted Prefectas, leap from the saddle and engage you in an action-packed fire-fight.

	SKILL	STAMINA
SCOOTER PILOT	7	8
SCOOTER TROOPER	8	8

If you win, turn to 280.

123

After a while, the ivory horn blows no more. Marsatu, believe it or not, now appears a little reticent, perhaps ashamed for having murdered his creator. But he notices you glancing at him. 'What are *you* staring at?' he snaps, peeved. He shoves you off balance; you stumble against the cell bars and are vaporized.

124

You pass into a storage room which is filled with electronic gadgetry, gas cylinders, flame torches and many other useful pieces of equipment. A noise makes you spin around and to your horror you discover a blob slithering through the hole behind you – the remains of a spacesuit still clinging to its tacky surface. You must vacate this room – but first you just have time to grab two of the following items, which you may find useful later on.

> electrostatic inducer
> flame torch
> oxygen cylinder
> laminex sheet
> 3-D pictoscope
> viscous negator

When you have settled on two objects, add them to your *Adventure Sheet*, then you may exit through a round aperture in the opposite wall (turn to 379), or climb a ladder to the level above (turn to 9).

125

You have come perilously close to the huge spaceship. At the last moment, you swing your own craft into a desperate manoeuvre to avoid collision. *Test your Luck*. If you are Lucky, turn to 206; if you are Unlucky, turn to 383.

126

Unluckily for you, the blob's superb driving skills enable it to dodge your abandoned vehicle. Just as it

126

is about to pounce on you, you notice an open side-hatch through which you fling yourself into a long chamber. It is filled with shelves containing food, eating and drinking utensils, and hundreds of tables and chairs: the space station's main refectory. The blob is close upon your tail as you run towards a revolving doorway at the other end of the room (blobs can't get through revolving doors – you hope!). You barely have time to grab a couple of the following items as you run.

> chair
> blancmange
> carving knife
> leg of mutton
> teapot
> cinnamon stick

Choose two items and add them to your *Adventure Sheet*. When you reach the revolving door, will you swing it clockwise (turn to **9**), or anti-clockwise (turn to **103**)?

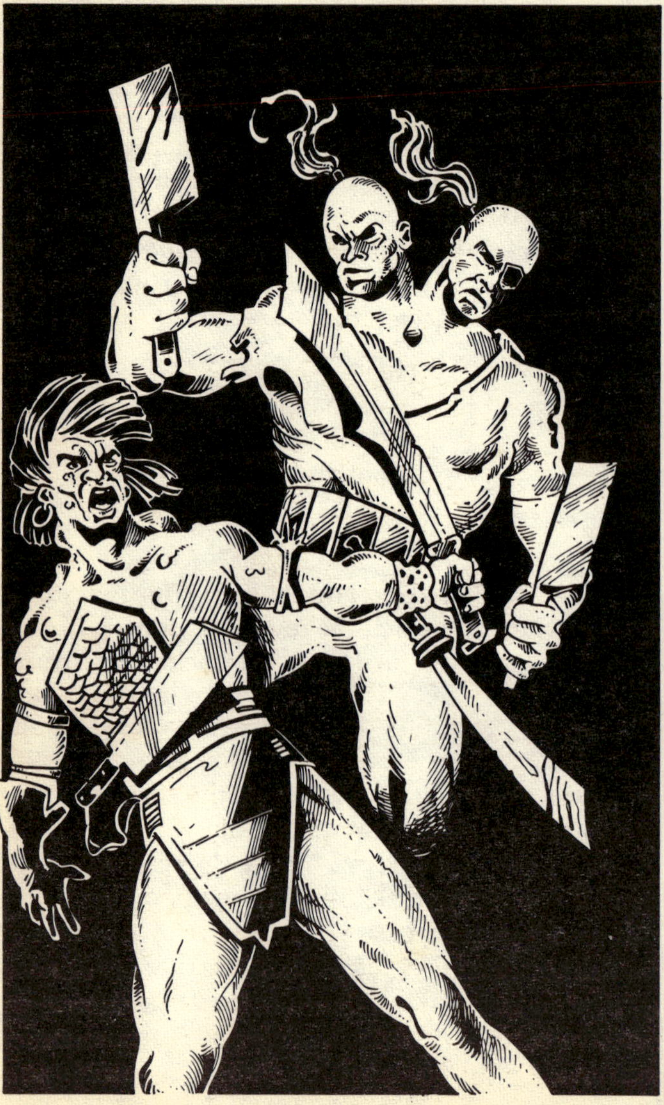

127

Both Brutes scream and charge at you with meat cleavers and scimitars.

	SKILL	STAMINA
RED-NOSED BRUTE	5	14
WARTY BRUTE	6	8

If you win, turn to **221**.

128

There is a huge blast overhead as a nuclear mini-charge explodes. Deduct 2 points from your STAMINA. Hastily, you abandon the crippled ship, and jump into the swamp. Luckily, Central City is now only a few miles away. Even closer is a concrete launch wharf, with a hover-ship moored alongside, and a tubeway building. A group of octopoidal dignitaries have recently disembarked from the ship, and are making their way towards the building. Will you approach the building (turn to **17**), or the hover-ship (turn to **211**)?

Zud is delighted. At a command from him, his machine's grabbing arm retrieves a key from a secret compartment, unlocks Gnasha's cylinder, and extracts it from your chest. (Remove Zud's cylinder from your *Adventure Sheet*.) Next, the arm snatches the Bicephalon's brain and inserts it into a small black box beneath Zud's leather seat. Another Bicephalon brain, old and withered, is taken out and thrown to the floor. Zud now sneers contemptuously at you. 'I need the brain to control this machine, for it to understand my commands and obey them. My own withered body is naturally quite useless, and the machine carries out all my functions, even helping me to speak and breathe. As the old brain was tiring, I needed another one quickly, and now I've got it! Ha! I'll show you just how strong I am now, by crushing you like a fly!' The machine rolls forward, raising a metal arm. Will you dive towards the open doorway (turn to **94**), or jump on to a desk and draw your laser-sword (turn to **151**)?

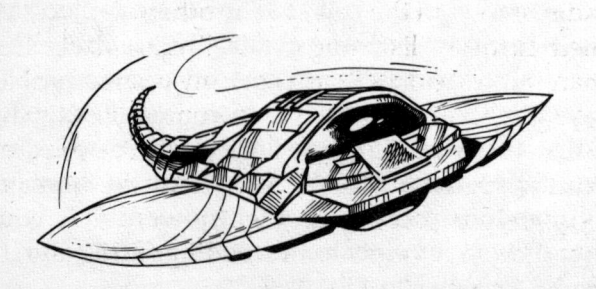

130

Epicurien the Torturer works on you all day, extracting information piece by agonizing piece, until you lapse into unconsciousness, never to awaken again.

131

Reduce your oxygen supply by 3 points, and deduct 1 point from your STAMINA. Although your idea is sound, Farkin had anticipated this. He kicks the pistol from your hand, just as you are about to fire. Will you:

Try a neck-chop?	Turn to **105**
Try an upper-cut?	Turn to **45**
Head-butt Fog Farkin?	Turn to **207**

132

'Wait!' you cry, breaking open the sphere and offering them the headset. 'If you don't blab, I'll give you this!' Luckily for you, the Yappies have never seen a headset before, so they stay to examine it. First, you place it on Zap's head and tune it in to the funkiest radio-station in the galaxy. The other two soon take their turns in listening. 'Wow!' cries Zap. 'Cool, man-thing!' shouts Brag. 'Rock my cosmic marbles!' says the third, slapping his companion's paws. 'This is terrifico! OK, we'll keep the beat box, and you can space out o' here.' You vacate the laboratory as quickly as you can, and return to Vault 6, where you hide in a ventilator shaft. The fun is about to begin! Turn to **187**.

133
Test your Luck. If you are Lucky, turn to **157**; if you are Unlucky, turn to **27**.

134
Heat is 'solid' in the 17th dimension, so, rather than killing the warrior, you have merely tied it up in a mass of long, silvery laser-cords! Now you have leisure to examine the basement in some detail. You walk around the walls, now and then sticking your head through to see what is beyond. There also appears to be another level below the basement. If you wish to examine this, turn to **86**; if you prefer to pass through a wall into another room, turn to **174**.

135
You are caught in a pulser beam. Reduce your SHIELDS by 1 point *permanently*. Now, your situation is:

Starspray: Pitch +54 ... Roll +82 ... Yaw −5 ...
Enemy: Pitch +35 ... Roll +60 ... Yaw +13 ...
Relative speed 1000 ...

Will you:

Maintain speed, pitch +20?	Turn to 366
Halve speed, pitch +80?	Turn to 312
Accelerate to 2000, pitch +50?	Turn to 269

136

The crew manage to repulse the attackers after a fierce struggle. But your ship is crippled and must soon put you down to lighten its load. Turn to 32.

137

Ahead of you rears the dark hull of a gigantic revolving space station. Peculiarly, it is emitting a series of radio signals which, apart from a distress code, you are unable to interpret. You decide to dock there, but as you approach you are confronted by a lightweight auto-drone. The drone's function is to protect the station from intruders such as yourself!

AUTO-DRONE RATING 6 LASERS 4 SHIELDS 7

If you win, turn to 71.

138

One of the most useful tricks you have learnt is how to feign death. Now, you hold your breath, slow your heartbeat and lower your body temperature so much that you do indeed appear stone dead! The spider-guard is almost as mortified as you are. 'No, this can't be!' it squeaks. 'I didn't hit him *that* hard!' The spider performs a wild dance of frustration, before scuttling off to summon its companions. These arrive shortly and slit open your cocoon to check your heartbeat. 'Fool!' one of them says to your guard. 'You *have* killed him! Now we'll have to eat him before he's been properly stewed; that delightful, subtle flavour will be lacking! Bah, when the Queen finds out, you'll suffer for it!' After a struggle, the guard is overpowered and dragged underground to a horrible fate. Mercifully, you have been left alone – and free! Turn to **114**.

139

'Durnng, huh?' you reply in a daze, as the Deik calls you over again. Now he is furious. 'So, we've got a moron to contend with, eh? OK boys, show him the door!' Two brutish Hulks appear from behind the bar, seize you and beat you insensible, before throwing you out. Deduct 2 points from your STAMINA. 'And you'll stay out, if you know what's good for yer!' With Gnasha gnawing away inside you and no hope of recovering the Bicephalon's brain, your fate seems sealed. Dejectedly, you decide to forget about Zud and his task, and continue with your own mission – while you have time. Turn to 7.

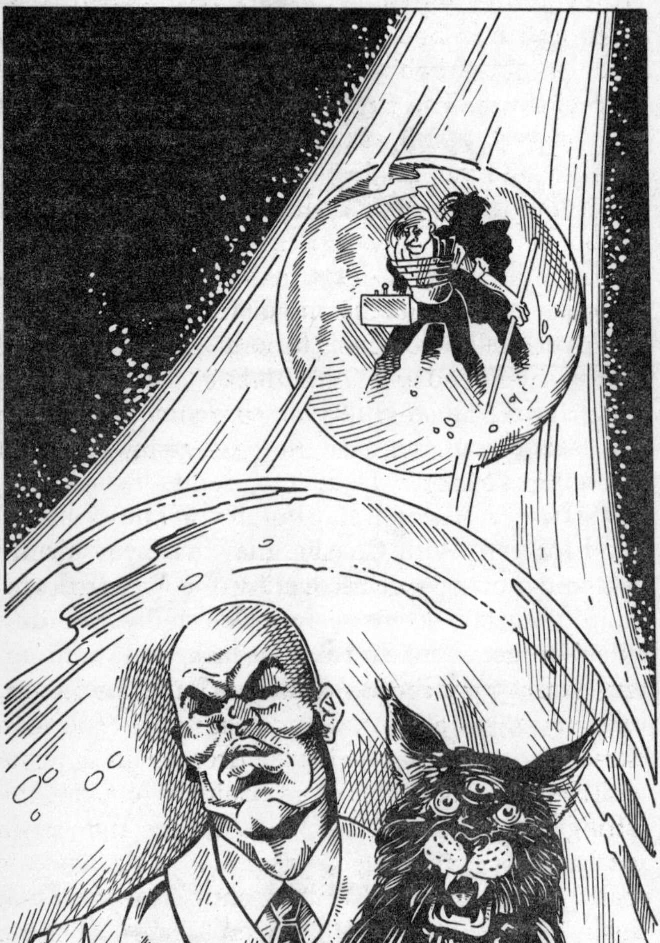

140

You continue for some distance past arched passages and iron-bound doors. Then suddenly you hear a noise behind you: two bubble-cars are approaching. The first contains a purple-skinned man in a white suit, stroking a three-eyed black cat. The second car holds two green-skinned Brutes with long noses and thick, pudgy hands holding clubbers: long poles with mechanically operated wood-and-leather cudgels on their ends. Each Brute is protected by a suit of banded iron. When they see you, the man in the first car yells: 'You there, halt! Master and Woderwick command!' The two Brutes leap from their vehicle. Will you try to outrun them (turn to **339**), or kneel in the passage and shoot at them (turn to **287**)?

141

This manoeuvre showed real flare! Turn to **206**.

142

You hear music coming from a room in the manor, so you creep to a window and peer inside. You see a strange, purple-skinned man dressed in a white suit; he is sitting on a stool and daintily plucking the strings of an electric balalaika. Beside him, on a cushion, is a three-eyed black cat. Your view is partly obscured by a window shutter, and so you hear, but do not see, a door open to one side of the room. From this a gruff voice speaks: 'We've looked everywhere, boss, but cannot find it.' The purple-skinned man glances at the cat and then back to the door. 'Send for Epicurien, then, and we'll soon know,' he replies. The door slams shut. Now, will you approach the front entrance (turn to **239**), or, if you haven't already done so, approach the nearest tetrahedron (turn to **57**)?

143

After a moment, there is a bright flash to your left. Several Valioog starfighters are incinerated in a massive fireball, and even your own craft is damaged; reduce your SHIELDS by 1 point *permanently*. Will you now commence a strafing run on the Valioog mothership (turn to **369**), remain at distance and scan the enemy craft (turn to **215**), or risk switching on the nuclear accelerators (turn to **292**)?

144

'Wonderful!' Sam exclaims. 'You see, L' Bastin sent a diabolical creature, a Kanberran Mogs monster, to kill me. It would have got me soon, too, but for your generous offer of help.' Sam now leads you to an old iron barge hidden among the reeds. 'The Mogs monster dwells on a barge, somewhat similar to this, in the middle of the lake. If you take this boat out now, you may catch it unawares. Of course, I would do this myself except, well, I lack the heart for fighting. It was not built within me, so to speak!' Somewhat flustered, you heave your craft into the lake, preparing for your assault. Turn to **353**.

145

You board an unoccupied tube-car and leave for the city. Unluckily, you meet another carriage coming down the tube from the opposite direction. There is a terrific blast as the two vehicles collide, and you are thrown forward. Deduct 4 points from your STAMINA. In a daze, you scramble from the wreckage, along the tube and into the city. Turn to **323**.

146

The lasers crackle, and the water beneath Mogs' ship sizzles and steams: you fired too low. Mogs prepares to retaliate as you adjust your aim.

	RATING	LASERS	SHIELDS
MOGS' CUTTER	9	3	10
YOUR OLD BARGE	–	3	7

If you win, turn to **69**.

147

'You lazy, fat thing!' you yell back. 'I hope you're eaten by your queen; I bet your father was!' Unluckily for you, the last comment is indeed true. The spider is most infuriated, and beats you to death with a rock.

148

Your ship is scarred by a scintillating, multi-coloured ray. Reduce your SHIELDS by 1 point *permanently*.

Starspray: Pitch +36.5... Roll +112...
Yaw −5...
Enemy: Pitch +35... Roll +60...
Yaw +13...
Relative speed 2000...

You may:

Maintain speed, pitch 17.5, roll 112, yaw −5	Turn to 336
Halve speed, pitch 2.5, roll 30	Turn to 366
Accelerate to 4000, pitch 5	Turn to 248

149

As you touch the hemisphere, a coloured streak of light shoots from it towards the floor. The light-ray gradually forms into a little holographic creature who, strangely, begins to recite the ship's battle procedure plans. The hemisphere is obviously an information storage bank. You listen for some time, '... and finally,' recites the little creature, 'action plan number 368: suicide strategy, employing a ten-megaton bomb.' The holograph disappears. As the hemisphere may provide you with useful information later on, you wrap it up and put it in your pocket. (Add the ionic sphere to your *Adventure Sheet*.) Now if you have not done so already, you may examine the multi-armed robot against the wall (turn to **304**), or the unmarked wooden crate (turn to **255**).

150

Glip now turns the red ring one segment anti-clockwise, but his path is blocked by a screen. Scuttlebug rotates the blue ring one segment clockwise, and he too is foiled. Finally Mutant turns the yellow ring one segment anti-clockwise, but his phase ends. The third move begins. Will you rotate the red ring one segment clockwise (turn to **58**), or two segments anti-clockwise (turn to **153**)?

151

'Rise!' commands Zud to his machine, intending to climb on to the desk and seize you. Surprisingly, however, the craft responds by jerking around crazily, spinning like a top, and trying to climb the walls – obviously you must have injured the Bicephalon's brain when you trod on it. Before Zud can gain control, you try a command of your own: 'Fold!' The machine immediately responds, by collapsing to the floor and folding its peculiar metal arms and legs. Then it sparks and seizes up entirely, trapping Zud. He is in a rage as you search his chambers, looking for a plan or key which will help you to gain access to Vault 2. Unluckily, you find neither, so you steal a bottle of acid in payment for all your troubles (add this to your *Adventure Sheet*), and depart the chamber. Turn to **25**.

152

The bowl you are standing in fills with fire. You dance a not-too-merry jig, as does Dr Strangething. Deduct 5 points from your STAMINA. Eventually the fire dies down. If you are still alive, you may continue through the passages. Turn to **200**.

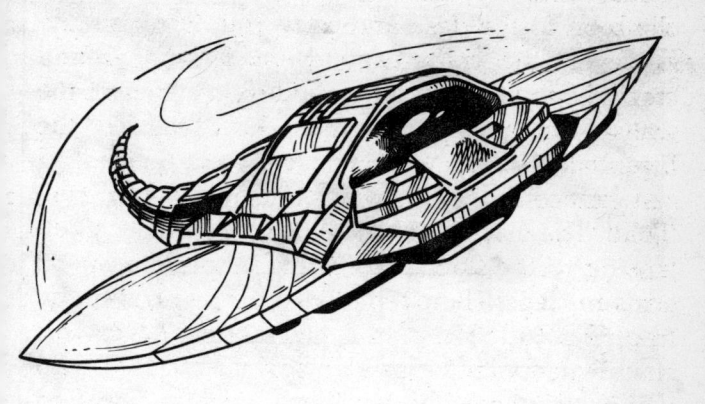

153

Glip now turns the red ring one segment clockwise, and has an unobstructed path. Aiming an electro-lance, he charges on his armoured steed into your rear. You are unable to bring all your weapons to bear on him in time.

	RATING	LASERS	SHIELDS
GLIP	4	3	8
GRASSHOPPER	–	2	10

If you win, another Glip appears on the vacated segment on the red ring. Next, Scuttlebug rotates the blue ring one segment clockwise. Finally Mutant rotates the yellow ring one segment anti-clockwise, and the third move ends. Now, will you rotate the red ring one segment clockwise (turn to **106**), or two segments anti-clockwise (turn to **299**)?

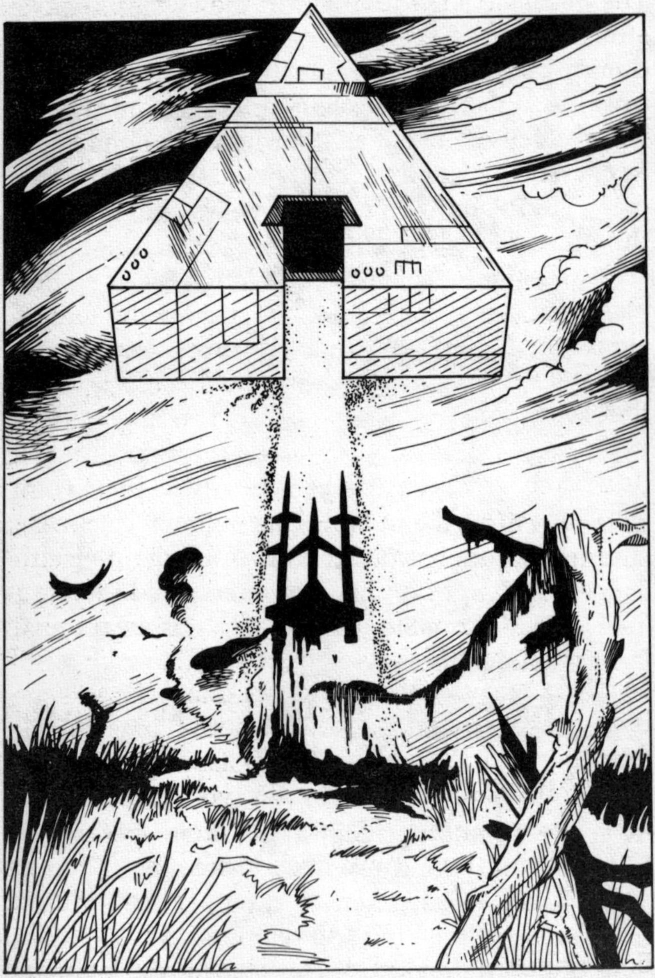

154

The *Starspray* jerks to a halt in the swamp, smoke streaming from the damaged port engine. Abandoning your craft, you wade through the thick ooze towards a gnarled tree, half a mile distant. Just as you reach it, you spot an enormous triangular ship approaching from the city. It hovers over your own craft, picking it up on a tractor-beam, and releasing three small scoutcraft before departing. The scoutships, a rocket scooter, a long-legged spider-craft and a swamp-yacht, are ridden by broad-shouldered, dog-headed warriors: obviously Prefectas. They are searching the swamp for you; the scooter and the spider-craft are heading towards your tree. Will you attempt to fight the spider-craft (turn to **68**), capture the scooter (turn to **122**), or climb the tree (turn to **165**)?

155

You take a sip. It seems pleasant enough, quite refreshing in fact. You begin gulping greedily until Marsatu, overcoming his astonishment, knocks the bowl from your hands. 'No, no!' he exclaims, 'that is *foot* ointment. You have just poisoned yourself!' Suddenly, your stomach cramps, your mind swirls, and you pass out. Deduct 4 points from your STAMINA. If you are still alive, turn to **54**.

156

Breaking open the globe, you recover the jet boots and try them on. Then, lighting their fuses, you wait for the spurt of flame to rocket you skywards.

Unfortunately the boots are faulty. One is sluggish and drifts left; the other, though leaking badly, is much faster and pulls right. For a minute you leap and flip dizzily through the air, out of control. Then, when you manage to steer yourself downwards and land beside Marsatu at the dome's entrance, one of your boots explodes. Your legs are badly burned. Deduct 4 points from your STAMINA. Marsatu, whose cloak has been singed by the accident, is furious. 'Look at my robe. It cost me four credits, and now it's useless!' Screaming insults, he beats you repeatedly with a short staff until, finally, he calms down. Turn to 363.

As you had hoped, the quill belonged to a brown-tailed Raccoot, a creature found in huge herds on Aarok. The quills contain powerful acid; now you put it to good use by dripping it on to your bonds. Although you singe your fingers (deduct 1 point from your STAMINA), you successfully break free and rush at the dozy spider-guard.

SPIDER-GUARD   SKILL 6   STAMINA 8

If you win, turn to 114.

158

Brac's laser fires and misses you, but you jump left and roll into Bric's line of fire. 'Now just you wait, Brac,' says Bric. 'How do you know he's a . . . vstirx . . . tsanngyx . . .' After a moment's buzzing, Brac moans. 'All right, ask him your question, Bric, but I bet he doesn't know.' Now Bric pipes up, 'Stranger, if friend you be, answer us: who is Head?' Will you answer:

Brac?	Turn to 111
Rhio?	Turn to 59
Jabob Neror Chintifox the Third, (the buggy's maker, whose name is stamped on a metal plate on the front fender)?	Turn to 49
The bell-craft's spherical computer?	Turn to 194

159

You punch a Prefecta in the face and twist yourself free. But another Prefecta, quick to react, produces a stun-stick, which he whirls at you, knocking you down with its powerful electrical charge. Deduct 2 points from your STAMINA. Marsatu cackles: 'You see, it is futile to attempt to escape from my wise master's creations.' The Prefectas pick you up again, and you proceed along the hall. Turn to 322.

160

The street soon becomes a dirt track which, by the middle of the afternoon, peters out altogether. For the past few hours you have been heading through rugged ashlands towards a ridge of red moonstone, bordering the valley. You are beginning to doubt that you will ever get out of the valley, let alone off this miserable planet... Eventually, however, you do reach the ridge and, rounding a rocky jut, discover a forking path. One trail leads left towards a spiny ridge (turn to 354), the other twists right (turn to 307); or you may wish to work your way along the base of the hill (turn to 375).

161

As you step on to the plaque set in the floor, mysterious fiery letters arise from it:

A voice translates: 'Central Vaults Ahead.' You may wish to copy the letters on a piece of paper; and remember the words, as they may be useful later on. Then you continue along the passage. Turn to 241.

162

At a single command from its owner, Zud's machine knocks the pistol from your hand, picks you up by the heels, and metes out a sound thrashing. 'Sheer insolence!' Zud rebukes. 'You cannot defeat me, as you now plainly see. So, will you help me?' Mournfully, you agree. Turn to **315**.

163

After a moment, your visual display console flashes with the message: 'Weak spot located on enemy port retro vent 5'. Do you wish to examine the Valioog's port vents using the image intensifier scanscope (turn to **215**); switch on an anti-detection device, if you haven't done so already (turn to **70**); switch off thrusters and glide towards the enemy (turn to **121**); or dart towards the Valioog at Mach 6 (turn to **369**)?

164

You manipulate your ship's controls and enter the 4th dimension. Outside, colours swirl and clash as you time-warp towards Aarok: it will take about six minutes 'real time' to reach the planet. After two minutes, however, you notice a fuzzy purple blotch spreading over your starboard thruster. It is some kind of space-weed which is growing rapidly in the fertile time-warp energy field. If it is allowed to spread further, it may choke the thruster and destroy your spacecraft; on the other hand, a premature jump into 'real space', which would enable you to cut the fungus off, could also prove perilous. So, will you ignore the fungus and continue towards Aarok (turn to **346**); or exit the time–space warp, in order to leave the ship and cut the growth away (turn to **62**)?

165

Most surprisingly, as you attempt to climb the tree, a siren sounds and a huge bell-shaped vessel thrusts itself up from the murky swamp. On its top, an iron lid slides open and a voice calls beckoningly to you: 'Hoi, yoi hoi! This way!' Peculiarly, the Prefecta in the spider-craft remains at a distance, cackling profusely. Do you wish to escape into the bell-ship (turn to **29**), or try to capture the spider-craft (turn to **68**)?

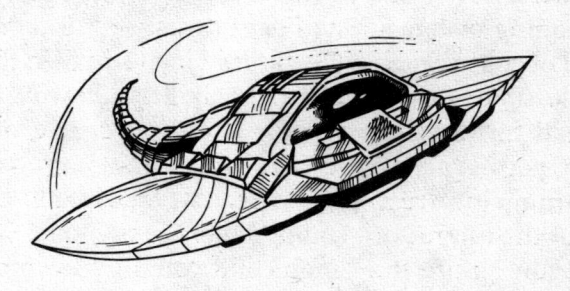

166

The man in the white suit, Woderwick, and the three-eyed black cat have been watching the fight from the safety of their bubble-car. Now Woderwick screams, 'Those widiculous cweatures! Well, I'll show him.' Woderwick aims a cone-shaped device at you. Many scintillating, rainbow-coloured strings branch out from it, hitting you and knocking you unconscious. Turn to **237**.

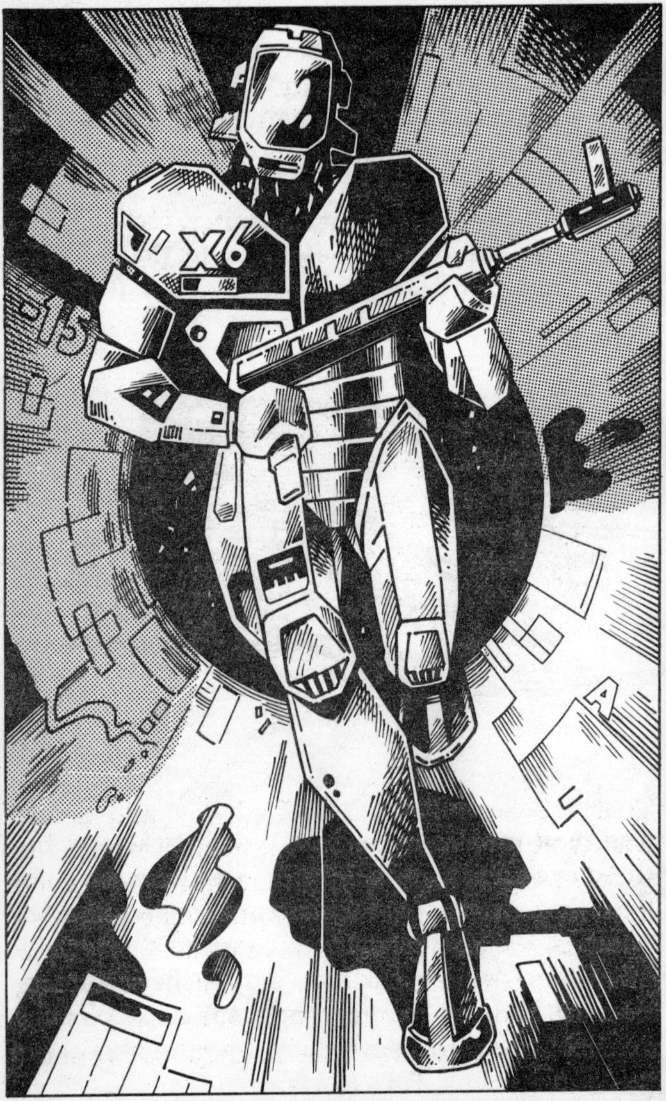
X6
15
A

167

You dash along a sloping passage, but are pursued by a faceless defence Cyborg – which catches up with you in no time at all. Now you must defend yourself.

CYBORG   SKILL 8   STAMINA 10

If you win, turn to **173**.

168

'Alas!' replies Marsatu. 'Though I would dearly wish it otherwise, I am a businessman by nature. As such, I cannot return your money in whole, or even in part.' Jym is growing irritated. 'Come on, then! Time is money, and my time is valuable. Shell out or clear off!' You will have to attempt to sweet-talk Jym into helping you for free (turn to **195**), or fight him and try to operate the Roundabout yourself (turn to **67**).

169

When you arrive at the launch wharf, you abandon your craft. You notice that a group of octopoidal dignitaries have disembarked from the hover-ship and are moving slowly towards the tubeway building, flanked by lion-masked guards. Will you approach the tube station (turn to **17**), or the hover-ship (turn to **211**)?

170

Passing before her bow, you fire the lasers at the wheelhouse. A direct hit results, smoke billows, and molten metal flies in all directions. Mogs, screaming with rage, appears on deck, to leap behind a twin-barrelled laser.

	RATING	LASERS	SHIELDS
MOGS' CUTTER	9	2	10
YOUR OLD BARGE	–	3	7

If you win, turn to **69**.

171

For hours now, the lumps on your cheeks and thighs have been growing. Suddenly you pass out, as spasms of pain rack your body. When you awaken you find you have mutated into one of Schaine's hideous creatures. And she is leading you by a chain into the vast, crystal spaceship! Your adventure is over.

172

Your ship is hit by a salvo of air-torpedoes. Several crew are killed, and you are pierced by shrapnel. Deduct 6 points from your STAMINA. If you are still alive, turn to **329**.

173

The passage tapers down until it is less than four feet in diameter, then ends abruptly at a circular door secured by a security lock. Luckily for you, lock-picking was one of the skills you acquired at the space academy, so in very little time you open the door and enter an octagonal, rubber-floored room. Within, you find a number of motorized trolleys and outlandish three-wheeled scooters: obviously they are designed to carry the space station's heavy equipment from one place to another. Intrigued, you climb aboard a scooter and examine its controls. But you are distracted by a slobbering noise from behind. Turning, you are astonished to see a very hungry-looking orange blob rolling towards you. Since blobs are difficult to kill, you decide to vacate the room at once, using the high-powered scooter. You switch it on and throttle forward. Will you pass through the open double-doors ahead of you (turn to 219), or through the swinging doors on your right (turn to 266)?

174

Finding nothing of note in the room, you climb a flight of steps and, passing through a trap-door, enter the levels above. Turn to 385.

175

You withdraw the quills just in time, and save L'Bastin. However, Marsatu is more than a little peeved. 'He deserves death, and so do you!' he screams. With fists flailing, he lunges at you; but you manage to dodge sideways. Marsatu careers into the bars behind and disappears in a loud 'fupff'. L'Bastin moans his gratitude. 'You have saved me from that oaf, and in happier circumstances I would have rewarded you.' You help L'Bastin out of the tank and explain your mission to him. 'Alas, the defence computers are now beyond your reach,' he replies, 'even if you were free. But the Prefectas can be stopped in another way, which is this . . .' L'Bastin explains that, at present, he has produced only one batch of several hundred Prefectas, although another batch is under preparation in his vats in Vault 7. 'The first lot are impure: I accidentally spilt too much of one particular ingredient into their mixture. Although they do not realize it, it has made them haughty, overbearing and disloyal. If even more of the same chemical was added to the new batch, I am sure they would squabble among themselves, probably to our advantage. Unfortunately I have no more of the chemical left: I sprinkled the last of it on my dinner several days ago!' 'What *is* the ingredient, then?' you ask. 'Impure sodium chloride,' L'Bastin answers. Common salt! If you have any rock-salt, turn to **306**; otherwise, turn to **259**.

176

Your vessel rapidly sways from the path of a Deik lunge, then counter-attacks with a power-saw, which bites savagely through his hull. With a squeal, he cuts your saw blade pole with a steel snipper. Then his spiker punctures your ship, injuring you. Deduct 2 points from your STAMINA. Do you wish to:

Pull a scarlet nodule?	Turn to **264**
Ring a chime?	Turn to **372**
Squeeze a red jelly?	Turn to **314**

177

You close in on the flank of your prey.

Starspray: Pitch +21.5 . . . Roll +112 . . .
   Yaw +19.5 . . .
Enemy: Pitch +35 . . . Roll +60 . . .
   Yaw +13 . . .
Relative speed 2000 . . .

You may:

Halve speed, pitch +30	Turn to **231**
Halve speed, roll +30, yaw −10	Turn to **22**
Halve speed, roll +5, yaw −5	Turn to **203**

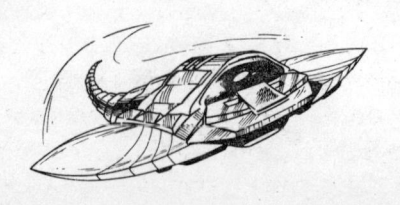

178

You must fight the spiders from a precarious position, so deduct 1 point from your SKILL temporarily during the following combat.

	SKILL	STAMINA
BROWN SPIDER	8	4
FAT SPIDER	7	4
SPINDLY SPIDER	6	6

If you win, turn to **273**.

179

You explain your mission to Rhio. He is most sympathetic and offers to lead you towards Central City; you readily accept. Manipulating the craft's controls, he submerges the huge bell and directs it northwards through the swamp, switching it to auto-control before reclining into a plush, feather-cushioned chair. 'I'm a little fatigued,' says the ageing Rhio. 'I'm afraid the excitement's been a little too much for me, and I must rest. However, if you wish to explore the lower levels of my ship, you're welcome to do so; you may even find some items of use to you. But be careful: some of the equipment may prove dangerous if handled improperly.' His head nods and soon he is fast asleep. Will you wait for him to wake up (turn to **296**), or will you explore the ship (turn to **392**)?

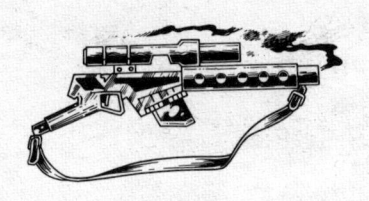

180

Reduce your oxygen supply by 4 points. Farkin is too powerful. You are unable to break his smothering grip. Will you:

Grope for your laser-pistol?	Turn to **131**
Try a neck-chop?	Turn to **105**
Trip Fog Farkin?	Turn to **207**

181

'No, thank you!' says Gnasha. 'My mother told me never to accept cold metal from a stranger! Besides, I am no longer hungry.' It leaves Epicurien and, bounding across to the door, slips through the iron grille and departs, leaving you to an unpleasant fate. Your adventure is over.

182

Unfortunately, before you reach Aarok, your communicator crackles with the voice of your leader, King Vaax. 'A slight detour, I'm afraid,' he says. 'Another urgent matter is before us. Within your vicinity is a Starfire Valioog; you must destroy it before it sun-homes. That is all!' Starfire Valioogs, you recall, are elusive fighting ships from the 57th dimension. They are enormous, immensely powerful, almost invincible: a fearsome armada in one ship. Their purpose is to wage destructive war in the higher planes. They rarely enter the lower dimensions, but when they do, their sole purpose is to sun-home. In order to drive their massive engines, refurbish draining force-shields, and restock with plasma-bolts, Valioogs plunder enormous quantities of energy from stars, often sucking them dry and leaving barren husks or empty space behind. Turn to **56**.

183
The whining ceases, and there is an explosion as an invisible spectron-pellet explodes over your head. Deduct 2 points from your STAMINA. Turn to **243**.

184
Lying face downwards, you slip through the floor into the manor's basement: a high open area with a heavy stone floor and jutting pillars of cobalt and carbon. You are on the point of examining a pillar when a fuzzy black orb attracts your attention. It is an armoured being of the 17th dimension, and you have invaded its domain! Luckily, your laser's heat is effective against it.

	RATING	LASERS	SHIELDS
17th-D BEING	9	2	6
YOUR POLYARMOUR	–	2	9

If you win, turn to **134**.

185

Turn to **348**.

186

The barge, wobbling slowly, manoeuvres towards you. Twenty feet above, it hovers, and an enormous nose, perhaps two feet long, appears over its side, followed by a small, beady-eyed face. 'Ahoy there, stranger!' yells this creature, the captain. 'You seem an able-bodied soul! I'm short on crew; if you come aboard, I'm sure we could come to some arrangement: your labour in return for a passage to the distant city, perhaps?' A rope ladder is cast over the side. Will you climb aboard (turn to **364**), or decline the offer (turn to **20**)?

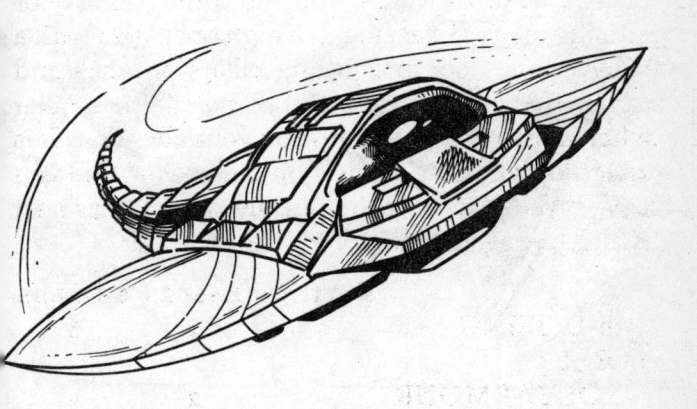

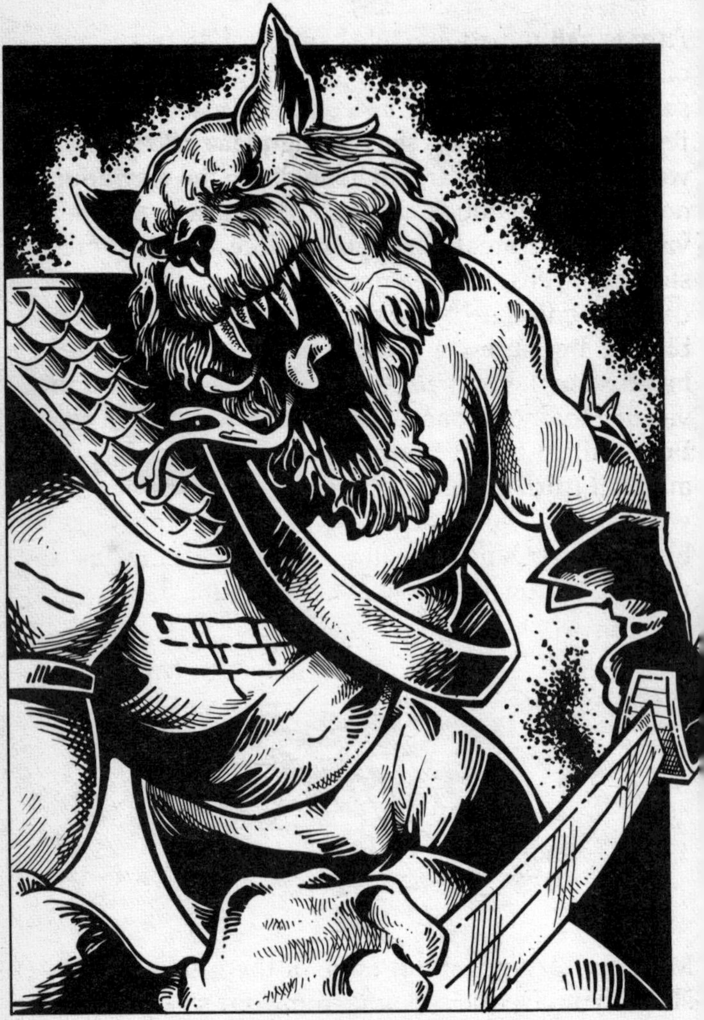

187

As you had hoped, the two batches of Prefectas, the old and the new, begin squabbling among themselves; soon fighting breaks out. You listen from the relative comfort of your hiding-place as the two warring factions charge up and down the corridors, down the air-tube, through the chambers and vaults. It is a great while before the sounds of fury subside. Venturing out, you discover a scene of dreadful carnage; bodies of hundreds of Prefectas, blasted by lasers or hacked to pieces by wicked implements, are strewn throughout the confines of vaults 6 and 7. In one room only do you meet a live Prefecta; it is badly wounded and will soon die. 'I am the last of my race,' it croaks. 'What an empire we could have built for ourselves! My strength ebbs, but if I am to die, I will go down fighting, as a warrior!' It attacks you with a sharp cutlass.

LAST PREFECTA   SKILL 6   STAMINA 6

If you win, turn to **400**.

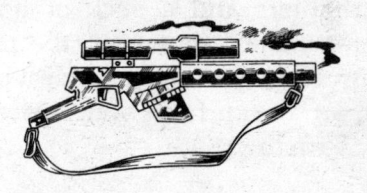

188

More Brutes appear, and one of them takes a pot-shot at you. Deduct 4 points from your STAMINA. If you are still alive, you are soon overwhelmed and captured. Turn to **367**.

189

The solvent is acidic, and burns your hands. Deduct 2 points from your STAMINA. Now, will you use the red solvent (turn to 324), or blast the rocky pillar with your laser (turn to 373)?

190

Suddenly a ship appears below. In every respect it resembles your own craft: it is your 'shadow', produced by the wondrous miracle of technology. The 'shadow' veers away, hotly pursued by small Valioog starfighters and a stick of homing torpedoes. Unfortunately, however, the fire in your rear laser turret has caused a great deal of damage. Remove the aft LASER from your spacecraft plan *permanently*. Turn to 43.

191

'Ya' *lie*, scint!' the old man barks, ''tis not ya' time, ha!' He punches you in the face and pushes you into your bowl. Several of the inn's other patrons, believing this to be jolly good fun, join in and try to drown you in the liquor, before you manage to overwhelm them and knock them cold. Deduct 3 points from your STAMINA. Unfortunately, the fracas has awoken the Deik, who now calls you over. Will you pretend to be a cretin and answer him stupidly (turn to **139**), or act like a rogue and answer him arrogantly (turn to **36**)?

192

The hatch explodes, blowing apart not only a large portion of the passage but yourself as well.

193

Tungsten-Klaw's grand ship is now very close. Your situation is:

Starspray: Pitch 0 . . . Roll +60 . . . Yaw 0 . . .
Enemy: Pitch +35 . . . Roll +60 . . . Yaw +13 . . .
Relative speed 1000 . . .

You may:

Maintain speed, pitch +35, roll +120, yaw +13	Turn to **141**
Maintain speed, pitch −35, roll −120, yaw −13	Turn to **383**
Maintain speed, roll −120	Turn to **125**

194

'Correct!' Bric replies. 'What do you . . .?' Bric's question is cut short by a suddenly blaring siren, and you must return hastily to the level above. Turn to **296**.

195

'Great giant, O most noble Jym,' you begin, 'indeed you are worthy of a generous fare. No doubt the Roundabout can only be operated by yourself: a character of great skills and cleverness of mind.' 'Duh, yep!' replies Jym, quite flattered. You go on grovelling for some time and have almost charmed Jym into providing a free fare when Marsatu chips in: '*Balderdash!* Jym, you are an oaf, and I am tired of having to pay your toll. You are a scoundrel and a knave to boot, and I have brought this gentleman along to do just that!' Jym erupts. Turn to **21**.

196

You push yourself and slide with increasing speed over the dome's steepening side. You hit the ground with a heavy 'thunk'. Deduct 3 points from your STAMINA. In a daze you look about you. Not far away, snickering at your misfortune, is Marsatu. Turn to **363**.

197

You pluck a piece of fruit and nibble daintily at it. Unfortunately, the plant to which it was attached is most angry at this, and wraps you in its thorny brambles. You must fight your way free.

BRAMBLES   SKILL 5   STAMINA 6

If you win, you may decide to eat some strawberries (turn to **362**), or follow a corridor leading from the hall (turn to **103**).

198

On a radarscope, you notice an enemy blip to the west disappear from view. Another blip which was approaching at speed from the north-west also vanishes after a huge explosion near by. But you are injured by flying glass and metal. Deduct 2 points from your STAMINA. Five more enemy ships appear on the screen: three in the south and two in the west. The computer suggests that you try one of the following manoeuvres:

Turn to port and fire an electrical
   charge on the ships to the south   Turn to **185**
Dive deep into the swamp   Turn to **290**

199

You activate the hemisphere, and ask it to compute your moves. It hums and buzzes, 'The most effective strategy for you will be to turn the red ring one segment clockwise on your first move, and two segments anti-clockwise in all your moves thereafter.' Turn to **345**.

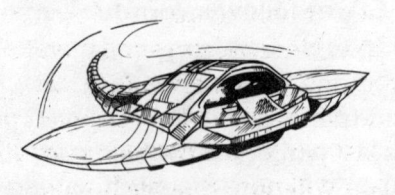

200

'Quick and careful, this way!' yells Dr Strangething as you follow him through the corridors into another room. The doctor points ahead. 'There is the way out,' he says gleefully. You see a glass tetrahedron on the other side of the room. 'But observe the tiles on the floor in front of us. Orange, green and blue circles and squares.' (Refer to *diagram 1* on the inside front cover.) 'You must be careful. There is only one way across. The tiles change colour as you step on them. Step on the wrong colour and you will be obliterated. However, the tattered vellum parchment you have recently picked up may provide you with a clue.' You step on the orange square tile C1, and all the square-shaped tiles change colour: orange to blue, blue to green, green to orange. The circles, however, do not change colour. *Note that in the following ordeal, if you turn to a paragraph which does not make sense in context, then you have stepped on the wrong tile and have been killed.* Will you now step on tile B1 (turn to **99**), tile C2 (turn to **365**), or tile D1 (turn to **73**)?

201

The fortress fades and the scenery changes dramatically. Now you are standing inside a small, transparent sphere, bobbing up and down in the middle of a deep lake. Near by, in a similar craft, is the Deik, flushed red and extremely angry. 'So, you passed the second trial and killed my beloved pet Jaj! Well, this is the last part of the contest; you will not find it so easy! You will note that each sphere has a small locked hatch. Also, as you see, each has numerous open vents, allowing water to enter – we are, in fact, slowly sinking.' The only way to escape from your sphere is to obtain the hatch's key, which is strapped to your opponent's sphere, and unlock it. Likewise, the Deik can escape only by taking a key from beneath your craft. To achieve this, both spheres are fitted with a grabbing arm, as well as a few weapons: power saws, atom lances, electrodes and shields, among others. These are operated by many weird controls within your craft. The Deik grins. 'As we're sinking, I'm afraid there isn't time to explain the controls, so you'll just have to do your best!' The cheat! Pulling a lever, the Deik lurches forward to attack, raising shields and probes. At no small disadvantage, will you:

Ring a silver bell?	Turn to **291**
Twist a spongy nodule?	Turn to **26**
Break a mauve crystal?	Turn to **234**

202
For several hours you follow the causeway: beyond esplanades overlooking oceans of space, past apartments with crystal walls and ivory colonnades, over streams of liquid gold. During all this time, colourful lanterns ascend towards the roof, changing hue and casting smaller, dark shadows across your way: mid-day approaches. Pausing for refreshment, you review your position. The dome is now about ten miles to your north: somewhat closer than before but, with your own path continuing south-west beyond sight, no more accessible. You sigh and,

deciding to return north-east, turn your back on the dome. Near by, upon a huge glass pontoon, golden chrysanthemums, white star-dews and crimson thunderheads bloom upon the banks of a sweetly smelling lake. How odd! Only now do you perceive the significance of the immaculate gardens and terraces you have been passing all morning. They have all been tended by someone – or something! Sense-sharpened by this thought, you suddenly detect a movement among the willow-reeds. A bright yellow eye unexpectedly appears. Almost simultaneously, a voice screams, 'Drop your weapons, four-arms, or you're charcoal!' Will you relinquish your weapons (turn to 252), or dive for cover, firing your laser (turn to 19)?

203

You are attacked by a small pirate launch which has been ejected from the *Grand Archipelago*'s hold.

PIRATE
  LAUNCH   RATING 5   LASERS 2   SHIELDS 6

If you win, you find that your rapid combat manoeuvres have placed you on a different attack angle to your target. Turn to 112.

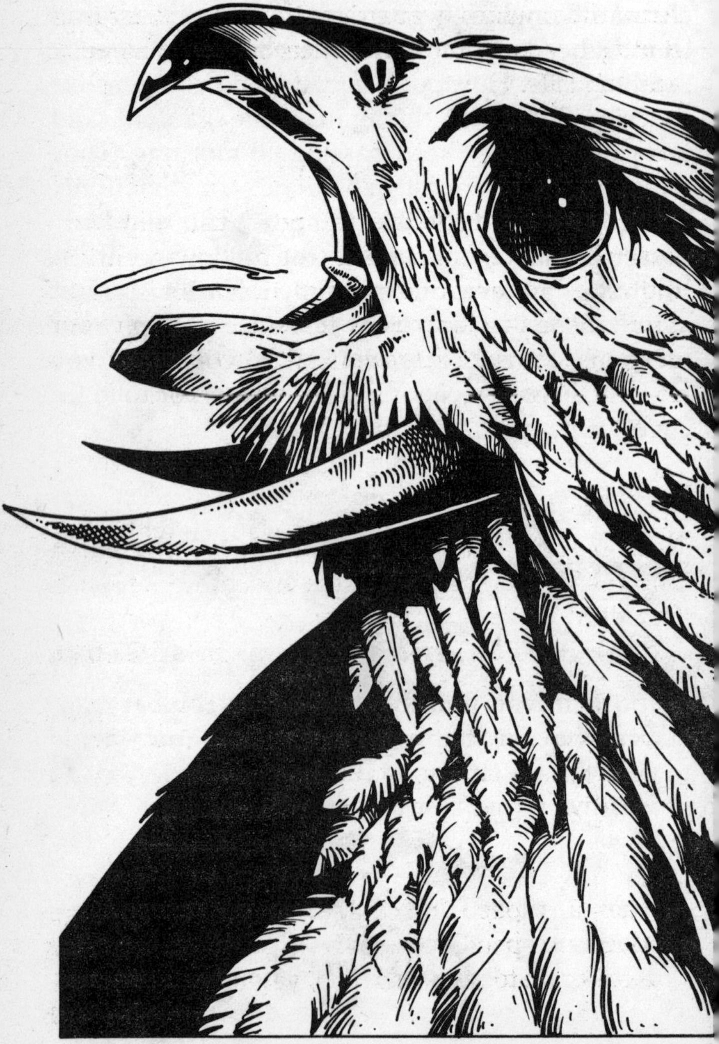

204

In Winsome's Way, you are cornered by a gruesome Armatilda, which is guarding its nest of fledglings. It attacks you with its enormous beak, talons, tusks and tendrils.

GRUESOME
    ARMATILDA   SKILL 9   STAMINA 8

If you win, you decide to spend the night in a deserted manor on the edge of the village. In the morning, you return to the junction with Spitflak's Street. Will you search the houses near by (turn to 380), or leave the village via Spitflak's Street (turn to 160)?

205

Your ship is jolted by a powerful electrical surge, and for a moment your lasers and computers malfunction. Reduce your SHIELDS by 1 point *permanently*. When your computers flicker on, the following data is before you:

Starspray: Pitch +19 ... Roll +82 ... Yaw −18 ...
Enemy: Pitch +35 ... Roll +60 ... Yaw +13 ...
Relative speed 1000 ...

Now, will you:

Maintain speed and course?	Turn to 34
Maintain speed, roll +60?	Turn to 135
Accelerate to 2000, roll +60, yaw −18?	Turn to 336

206

Your position, relative to the *Grand Archipelago*, is: pitch 0, roll 0, yaw 0: you are directly behind it! You fire your lasers at its most vunerable spot, and then roar away. Several seconds later the pirate's ship explodes in a massive fireball of heat and light. After a moment's jubilation, you switch back into time-warp, and continue on to Aarok, and your main mission. Turn to **279**.

207

Reduce your oxygen supply by 3 points. At the last moment, Farkin raises a leg and pushes you off-balance. Your move is ineffective. Will you:

Try a 'rabbit punch'?	Turn to **45**
Hit him with your buckler?	Turn to **357**
Trip Fog Farkin?	Turn to **120**

208

'Very well,' the speaker rings out, 'you have requested semi-automatic control of this ship. The recommendations I put to you are':

Spin south, laser-fire south	Turn to **348**
Spin east and fire-bomb west	Turn to **198**
Send out an auto-attack robot with a flame projector	Turn to **87**

209

You pass through the ovoid lock and remove your helmet. The air, although breathable, contains the faintest whiff of rocket fuel; it would seem that there is a leak somewhere, so you must be careful not to use your laser pistol or sword, for fear of sparking an explosion. Ahead of you, swaggering around a bend in the tubular passage, there now appears a human, dressed in a floppy blue corduroy cap and overalls; apparently a maintenance man. Beaming a broad smile, he leans forward to shake your hand. 'Welcome aboard the United Star-station *Diabolic-lese*. Barty Baxter at yer service!' There is something distinctly odd about him . . . In particular, his eyes are orange! Will you shake Barty by the hand (turn to **227**), or, distrusting him, hit him with the pommel of your laser-sword (turn to **300**)?

210

You plant your foot firmly on the face of the first spider; with a scream it loses its grip and falls to the ground with a thud. But its companions scuttle up quickly, tying you up in sticky webs. Soon you are lowered to the ground and dragged for miles across the desert, towards the spiders' camp. You arrive there at first light. Turn to **327**.

211

Surprisingly, the ship has been left unguarded. Relaxing behind the control panel, you steer it away from the wharf. Unluckily, an enemy skimmer-craft is approaching at speed.

	RATING	LASERS	SHIELDS
SKIMMER	3	5	8
YOUR HOVER-SHIP	–	4	10

If you win, turn to **101**.

212

With a clear path to you, the Scuttlebug attacks.

	RATING	LASERS	SHIELDS
SCUTTLEBUG	5	2	12
GRASS-HOPPER	–	2	10

If you win, turn to **258**.

213

There is an uncharted planet on your scanscope, at a distance of twenty-six million miles. Setting your controls for cruise speed, it will take you about five hours to reach it. On the way, you find yourself suddenly confronted by a broad, silver, sting-ray-shaped ship which has apparently just materialized from another dimension. It is the kind of ship often used by Pelhon Rangers, a band of misguided galactic vigilantes. You must defend yourself against this attack.

PELHON
  RANGERS RATING 5   LASERS 5   SHIELDS 8

If you win, turn to **14**.

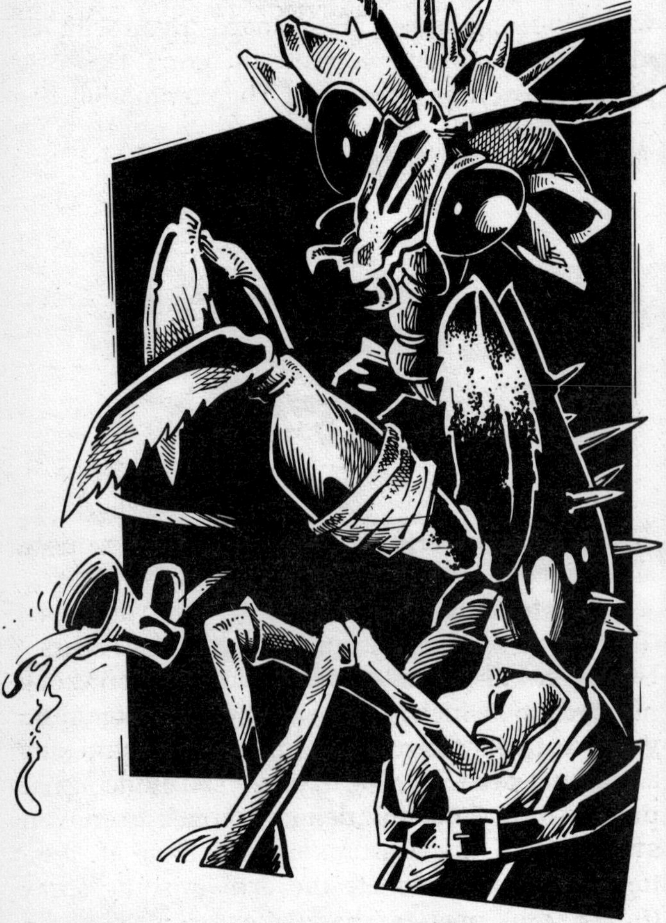

214

As you step up to the gong, you accidentally nudge a Red Manchurian, who spills his drink. For his woes, the long-limbed insect snaps at you with his mandibles, and hurls you into the gong. Deduct 2 points from your STAMINA. The commotion has awoken the Deik. Turn to **51**.

215

Using the scanscope, you visually locate the Valioog mothership's single weak spot, on the port retro vent. At this moment, your spaceship is struck by a plasma-pellet: reduce your SHIELDS by 1 point *permanently*, and deduct 2 points from your STAMINA. A fire has broken out in the aft laser turret. Will you activate the extinguishing spray (turn to **240**), operate 'shadow' electronic countermeasures (turn to **190**), or perform a complex roll manoeuvre (turn to **292**)?

216

The doctor continues: 'Anyway, what of yourself? My guess is that you're to be ransomed back to your family, though you'll probably arrive dead – or in pieces anyway!' At this instant, a squeaky voice can be heard from the other side of the door: 'Pieces enough, it's certain!' The door is opened, and in steps a hideous, corpulent figure with a squared-off blue beard and its head shaved except for a tiny dyed green tuft on top. Two large tusks protrude from its mouth. In one hand it holds the cell keys, in the other a wooden box filled to capacity with screws, metal knucklers, clubs, prods, probes and other devices of torture. 'I am Epicurien the Inquisitive, but *you* may call me sir!' He struts over to you, puts down his box, and grabs your hair. 'Right! I am curious. I have many questions. First, we'll have your name, your origin, and your intended destination. Then,' he says, fingering a curved knife, 'we'll send your family some material proof of your detention!' He pulls a chair up next to you and gropes for an implement in his box, while thumping your chest with his mallet-like fist. If Zud's cylinder is embedded in your chest, turn to **81**; otherwise, if you have a sensory capsule, turn to **229**; if you have neither of these, turn to **130**.

217

Your vessel is blasted by an atomic torpedo. Reduce your SHIELDS by 1 point *permanently*.

Starspray: Pitch +54 ... Roll +82 ... Yaw +3 ...
Enemy: Pitch +35 ... Roll +60 ... Yaw +13 ...
Relative speed 2000 ...

You may:

Halve speed, pitch +67.5, roll +30, yaw −3.5	Turn to **112**
Maintain speed, pitch +50, yaw −10	Turn to **177**
Maintain speed, pitch +52.5, roll +30, yaw +27.5	Turn to **285**

218

Sam's eyes flash with red. 'Very well, then. Clear off, or I'll turn *you* in!' Startled by his sudden change in mood, you step away, returning north-east along the causeway. At perhaps fifty paces Sam, now shrieking hysterically, fires his weapon at you. Deduct 1 point from your STAMINA. If you are still alive, you turn your back and flee. Turn to **318**.

219

You drive through the doors and up a long causeway. Unfortunately, the blob, which seems intent on having you for dinner, is still following, now on a motorized trolley. The creature is a skilful driver and is catching up quickly. You may wish to abandon your scooter and allow it to roll back down on the blob (turn to **126**), or decide to continue along the ramp (turn to **297**).

220

The whining ceases as an invisible spectron-pellet explodes in the middle of the passage. Deduct 4 points from your STAMINA. If you are still alive, turn to **243**.

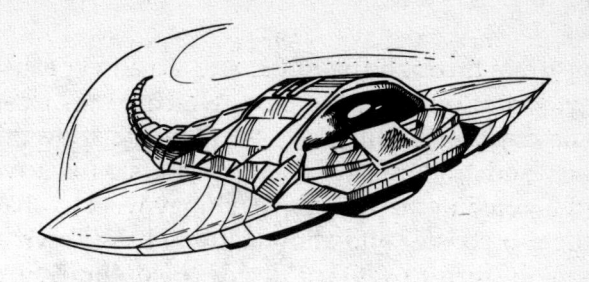

221

Dr Strangething throws down the arrow-shaped hour-hand. 'Quick, run!' Before you have time to move a muscle, Woderwick and Kogo have arrived in a bubble-car, attracted by the commotion. 'Ah! Ah!' says Woderwick delightedly. 'We never thought to examine the clock. Now the cursor is ours!' Woderwick aims a conical device at you. From it fly many rainbow-coloured strings which envelop you and knock you to the ground. The doctor looks on helplessly from the clock tower as Woderwick and Kogo saunter up to you and pick up the hour-hand. 'We'll dispose of you soon enough,' says Woderwick, 'but first for a spot of burglary!' Woderwick takes a crystal from around his neck. It expands and forms a lightly glowing ball around both man and cat. 'Now, go!' commands Woderwick, pointing the arrow slightly up and left. The pair vanish. Suddenly there is a loud scream from where they were standing, trailing off slowly to silence. The crystal reappears on the ground, but neither Woderwick, Kogo, nor the arrow return. Turn to **283**.

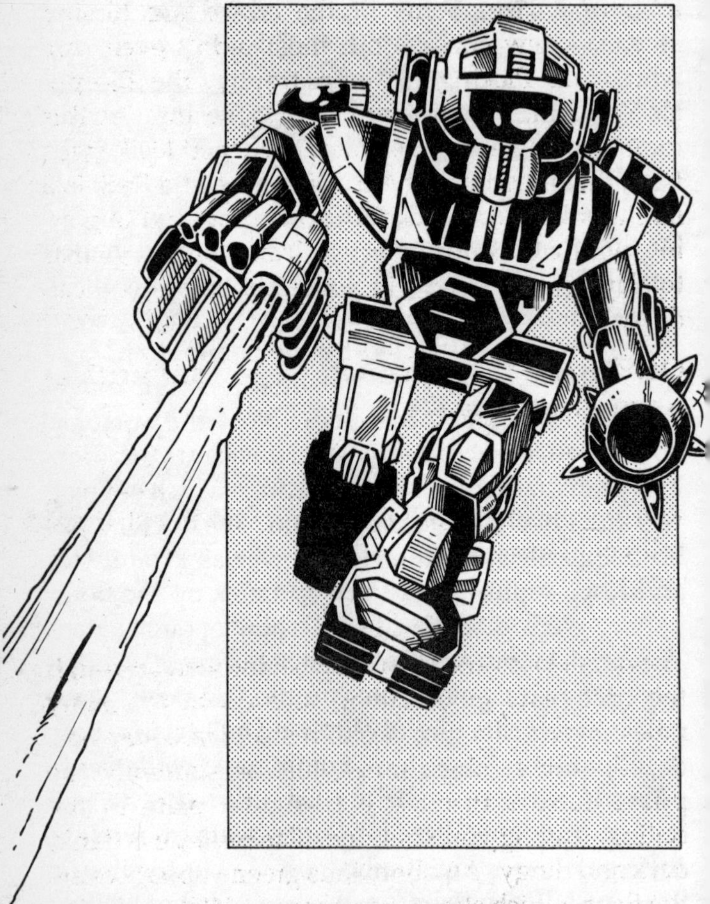

222

To the dismay of the inn's patrons, you step triumphantly from the orange sphere, returning rapidly to normal size. Some of the crowd are hissing at you, a few cheer – but most didn't even care who won. Picking up your trophy, the Bicephalon's brain, you prepare to exit the inn. At this moment, however, the water-drenched Deik steps from the hovering sphere. Of course, the Deik is a molluscoid and could not drown anyway! Shivering with cold and anger, he calls for his guards to slay you; one steps in your way before you can depart.

OGRE-OID   SKILL 6   STAMINA 14

If you win, turn to **119**.

223

Roll one die. If you roll 1, 2, 3 or 4, turn to **158**; if you roll 5 or 6, turn to **6**.

224

The door closes and the prism begins to fall through the base-plate in the floor, and down for many miles. Eventually it comes to rest and you step out, dazed, into a long tunnel. Just as suddenly the prism departs through a triangular plate in the ceiling, leaving you stranded. The passage is dank, dark and dingy. An obnoxious green vapour covers the floor, which slopes gently away. Will you go up the passage (turn to **140**), or down the passage (turn to **89**)?

Ignoring Marsatu's incessant blubbering, you examine your gaol. You are imprisoned in a cubic cage, the sides of which are precisely ten feet long. The bars, although thin and malleable, contain 'spike-hair', a scintillating electro-plastic charged to a million volts. Touch one and you will be vaporized. (The dust of a previous victim has not yet settled.) Upon the floor you find a tiny button, half melted and not easily identifiable – you recall similar buttons being worn by Bok, Marsatu's fish-faced servant . . . A quarter of an hour later, the warder returns with L'Bastin, still entombed within the posidon tank. The warder, a broad-faced Prefecta grinning like a cheshire cat, turns the power down to a mere hundred thousand volts and, with a pair of rubber-coated pliers, bends several bars apart. L'Bastin is wheeled in; when the bars have been bent back into shape, the warder turns the power up again. You had entered the cell in a similar fashion: the cage has no door. When the warder departs, Marsatu and L'Bastin begin to argue. 'I'm in a mess now, L'Bastin,' says Marsatu, 'and it's all *your* fault! You spent all your time designing those stupid Prefectas, when you could have been cloning hundreds of *me*! I told you so, but you wouldn't listen. Well, now we're all in this cell, and there's no hope. Really!' L'Bastin's voice reverberates from the ivory horn: 'Yes,' it drones, 'we're *really* in it. But what would I want with hundreds of copies of *you*? You were a disaster from the beginning; I put too much sawdust into your mixture, and it's all gone to your head! I should have melted you down, along with the other rejects!' In a fury, Marsatu pushes in every quill; the tinselfish go berserk and the oil turns red. Will you help L'Bastin (turn to **175**), or will you stuff your fingers in your ears and wait for the screams to subside (turn to **123**)?

226

You squeeze the laser trigger and roar away from the huge Valioog ship which, several seconds later, explodes in a ball of green flame, then crashes down into the nearby star, Cabrilow. You have saved the Cabrilowi solar system! Unfortunately, you have no time to celebrate, for you must immediately press on to Aarok, on your main mission. Will you time-warp (turn to **254**), or light-warp (turn to **279**)?

227

Removing a glove, you shake Barty's hand. At once, Barty transforms into his true self: a bright orange blob. Having an unrelenting grip on your hand, it wastes no time in rolling up your arm and devouring you piece by piece.

228

After you have zapped several spiders, the others beat a hasty retreat, to plan a new attack. You reach the top of the pillar, but you do not have to wait long before their next assault. This time there are many more, armed with hardy shields of interwoven webs, impervious to laser fire. *Test your Luck*. If you are Lucky, turn to **298**; if you are Unlucky, turn to **210**.

229

An idea springs to mind. You break the capsule, releasing the bitter chemicals. These greatly aid your telepathic powers, and you visualize an image of Woderwick entering the chamber. Epicurien, fooled by the image, looks up at him. 'Epicurien,' says 'Woderwick', 'there's been a terrible mistake. Release this humanoid immediately and give him his weapons back.' The torturer obeys without question. You are released, and are about to pick up your weapons when the vision fades. 'What is this,' says Epicurien, startled. 'A *trick*! I'll have yer!' He pulls a meat hook and prodder from his toolbox, leaps over a rack and attacks you.

| EPICURIEN | SKILL 7 | STAMINA 8 |

If you win, turn to **253**.

230

Luckily, there is a loose thread in your cocoon which you gradually begin to unravel whenever the guard turns his back on you. Eventually you wriggle out and charge the surprised spider. In the following combat, deduct 2 points from your SKILL temporarily, as you have no weapons.

| SPIDER-GUARD | SKILL 6 | STAMINA 8 |

If you win, turn to **114**.

231

After further drastic manoeuvres, your situation is:

Starspray: Pitch +20 ... Roll +30 ... Yaw 0 ...
Enemy: Pitch +35 ... Roll +60 ... Yaw +13 ...
Relative speed 1000 ...

Will you:

Maintain speed, pitch +55, yaw +13?	Turn to **248**
Maintain speed, pitch +55, roll +90, yaw +13?	Turn to **206**
Maintain speed, pitch +55, roll +30, yaw +13?	Turn to **193**

232

After a mighty tussle, you defeat the blob and jettison it into space. Then you destroy the space station. Will you continue towards Aarok in light-warp (turn to **182**), or in time-warp (turn to **254**)?

233

'A wise choice!' comments Marsatu. 'The spheres are skew-dimensional containers, warping volume as we know it. Break them at the appropriate time to receive your chosen items in full size. Now, we are good friends, yes!' You are not sure whether this is a statement or a question. In any case, before you can reply, Marsatu snatches your laser-sword and electro-javelin. 'An exchange of presents is a good feeling!' he cries. Deduct 1 point from your SKILL. Marsatu now leads you to his stables, where two bizarre mechanical contraptions have been saddled. One of these, an emerald-green machine resembling an enormous grasshopper, is for your use. The other, no less spectacular, is a gigantic metal turtle with a plush leather seat set high upon its shell. Marsatu sinks into it, declaring: 'Now we are almost ready to seek the Dome of Marvels and end your mission. The way is tricky, and I will guide you for a while – for a modest fee.' (Remove all your remaining credits from your *Adventure Sheet*.) 'Now, mount your grasshopper, and turn the controls thus and so, and we will be on our way!' Obeying Marsatu's commands, you steer your beast to the causeway, while Marsatu follows close behind. Turn to 333.

234

Your ship lurches forward and raises a plastic shield. The Deik, mastering his controls, moves just aft and starboard, then bears down on you, grabber raised and electrode buzzing. Examining your controls, will you:

Squeeze a green jelly?	Turn to 26
Break a yellow bulb?	Turn to 176
Do nothing?	Turn to 372

235

Before you manage to reach the wharf, you are set upon by a swift swamp-yacht.

	RATING	LASERS	SHIELDS
SWAMP-YACHT	4	3	6
YOUR COMBAT VEHICLE	–	2	10

If you win, you must abandon your vehicle. Will you turn towards a ventilator shaft in the nearby tubeway building (turn to **309**), or towards the building's main gate (turn to **397**), or will you head for the hover-ship, moored against the wharf (turn to **211**)?

236

'But I see that you have already met Schaine,' barks Krill, pointing at the widening gap on your forehead and the growing lumps on your face and legs. 'Come with me. It is not too late to reverse the transmutation process.' Krill leads you into a tiny chamber, far back in his cave, where he prepares a very special tonic. 'Take note,' he says, 'dew from an unripe cloudberry, picked at dawn . . . spleen of a devil-lizard albino of two seasons' standing . . . the first five leaves of a young ointbush, and water collected from the seven mystic rivers at Chochog: all blended in the prescribed manner and boiled in a gold-crystal vase for six minutes and twenty-seven seconds exactly!' You drink the bitter concoction, while Krill begins a low chant. When he has done, he continues, 'There, you will soon be cured. Of course, some would say that I have just performed magic, wizardry, or even witchcraft: Schaine herself calls it magic; but that is nonsense. I have merely utilized the laws of chemistry for preparing the correct medication; my chanting applied the rules of mathematics and physics to set up a resonance which would activate the compound in your body. These processes are no more magical than the ones you use to fly through space and time!' Turn to **341**.

237

Hours later, you awaken in a squalid brick cell. Your arms and legs are bound by steel cables and clamps to a low metal table. To one side, resting against the wall, are your weapons. On the other side are spiked seats, iron cages and other unimaginable devices with cogs, screws and pincers. You are in a torture chamber! A sniffle and a clanking of chains makes you raise your head. Looking past your feet, you notice, chained against the wall, a weird creature with a huge onion-shaped head and three tentacles. It is wearing, believe it or not, a white coat and spectacles. Its sparkly eyes are examining you. Its beaky mouth smiles faintly as it speaks: 'Good morning, stranger. This will be some day to remember, I can see that!' You strike up a light-hearted conversation with the creature. He is Dr Strangething, the owner of the manor-house you entered earlier. He was captured and imprisoned by Woderwick and his master Kogo, the three-eyed cat, a notoriously bad-tempered freebooter. 'Of course,' says the doctor, 'Woderwick is only Kogo's mindless familiar, through which the cat may communicate more readily with the humanoids. Woderwick's words are therefore those telepathically implanted by his master. Still,' muses the doctor, 'I believe there to be an imperfection in the transferral process, and that "Woderwick" should really be "Roderick"!' Dr Strangething tells you that he has been imprisoned for some days, beaten and tortured. 'I have invented a crystal, you see, that will enable a person to be transported almost anywhere instantaneously – if not sooner! Now *they* have it – Woderwick wears it on a chain around his neck; but they cannot use it. There is a cursor, you see – an arrow-shaped device which is needed to guide the crystal through space and time. Without it, the crystal is useless. I have hidden the cursor in my manor, but as yet neither Woderwick, Kogo nor their underlings have been able to locate it.' Turn to **216**.

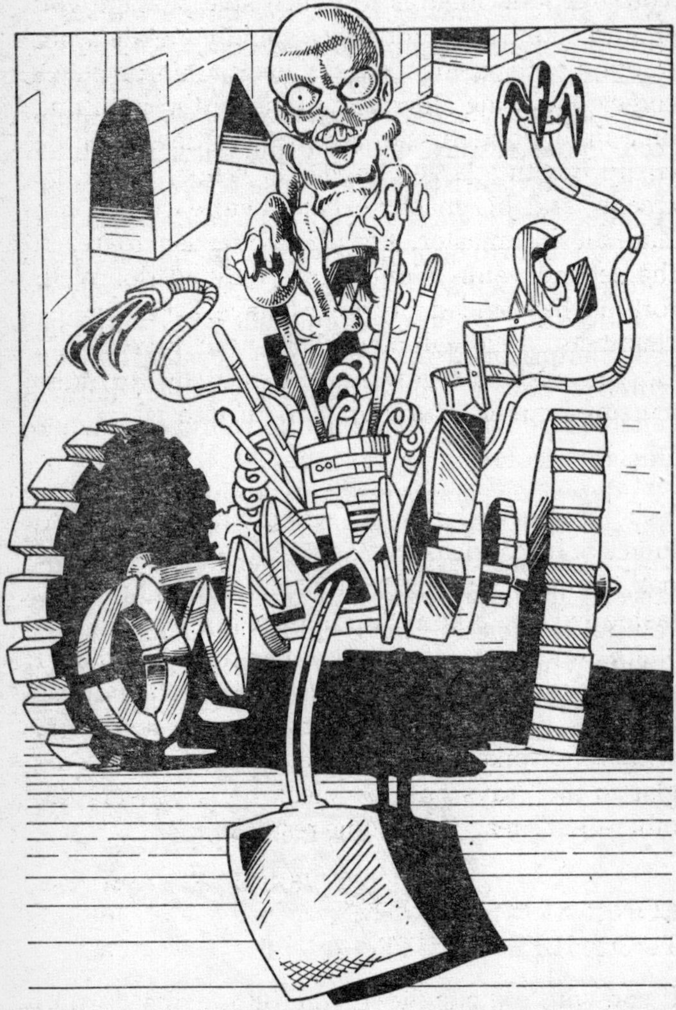

238

You are undecided as to which side-passage you should take when suddenly a spindly metallic contraption with springs, cogs, wheels and iron claws comes bounding along the tunnel. Atop it, sitting on a high wooden seat, is perched a decrepit little creature with a large blue head. 'Whoa, there!' he croaks, and his machine halts before you. 'I am Zud the lockmaster. Perhaps you wish to reach the second vault? Come now, they *all* do! Well, fortune has smiled on you. I have a key in my chambers which will help. Follow me, if you will.' Do you wish to follow Zud (turn to **16**), or, mistrusting him, go your own way (turn to **7**)?

239

You approach the door, wondering whether to knock or try to sneak in. You examine the door: solid oak, bound with iron. It has an iron knocker, fashioned like a lion. Suddenly it lunges forward, snaps, and bites off one of your fingers! Deduct 1 point from your SKILL. Now the door springs open, and two Brutes leap out, armed with revolvers, whips and spiked knuckledusters. 'Looks like a burglar to me!' says one. 'A sneak he is,' sneers the other. 'Let's teach him some respect!'

	SKILL	STAMINA
LONG-ARMED BRUTE	7	10
TOOTHLESS BRUTE	6	8

If you win, roll one die. If you roll 1, 2 or 3, turn to **272**. If you roll 4, 5, or 6, turn to **188**.

240

The fire is extinguished in a whoosh of gas. Unfortunately, while you were preoccupied with this task, a small Valioog sky-wasp has been released from the mothership, and has locked you into its sights.

SKY-WASP   RATING 6   LASERS 2   SHIELDS 8

If you win, turn to **23**.

241

The passage begins to descend gradually, and you find yourself at the entrance to a vast dark space, many miles wide and high. This is Vault 2. Within are scattered luminous, opaque tetrahedral prisms but, as you are not very close to any of them, it is difficult to tell their size. The only other source of light comes from a grand manor-house, with a steepled clock-tower, some distance away. Will you approach the nearest prism (turn to **57**), or seek the comforts of the manor instead (turn to **142**)?

242

You enter a triangular room with a sloping floor of green crystal. In the furthest corner there appears to be a small exit. Mounted on two of the walls are pegs, burdened by heavy spacesuits, helmets and face masks. One of the suits is oozing a luminous orange substance; from it the head of a man juts out. Slowly he swivels his head towards you, coughs several times, and grins wearily. 'I suppose you've come in answer to our distress signal. Well, you're too late! Most of the crew, perhaps all of them, have already been devoured by orange blobs. I'm being slowly eaten by one now! It's quite painless! I just wish you'd come along earlier and saved us. Never mind, I strongly recommend that you leave the station now – while you've still got a chance . . .' He coughs again, this time spitting orange bile. 'But here's a tip for you: don't use your lasers against them – there's a gas leak, and you'll be blown sky-high. If you're confronted by one, run away if you can, otherwise throw something at them. It'll take 'em a while to devour it and – if you're lucky – it may even kill 'em.' He closes his eyes and gets on with the business of dying. Will you return to the tubular passage and continue along it (turn to **173**), or will you leave via the small exit in the corner of the room (turn to **124**)?

243

Now you can hear the bandit laughing, further along the passage. There is also a loud click: he is loading another spectron-pellet into a projector.

Quickly you rush round the bend towards him. *Test your Luck*. If you are Lucky, turn to **343**; if you are Unlucky, turn to **331**.

244

You don a space suit and, harnessing a jet pack to your back, pass through the air-lock. Then, sidling across the fuselage, you push yourself across to the starboard retro thruster. The fungus is coarse and matted, and when you try to cut it with a laser-knife it turns quite hostile!

SPACE-WEED   SKILL 8   STAMINA 6

If you win, you decide to return to the ship, before the space-weed strikes again. Obviously the only way to dispose of it is to burn it off, while passing through a planet's atmosphere. Turn to **213**.

245

You peer warily at the spigot. Within it there appears to be a curled wire – possibly electrified. You decide to leave the spigot alone and continue down the corridor towards the exit. Turn to **257**.

246

You throw the sphere on the floor, expecting it to break open and reveal a magnificent suit of battle-armour. Instead, the sphere bounces away: it is made of rubber! Marsatu shrugs. 'An oversight on my part; not the genuine article, it seems.' Turn to **275**.

247

Test your Luck. If you are Lucky, turn to **158**; if you are Unlucky, turn to **6**.

248

You are blown to pieces by a huge nuclear mine.

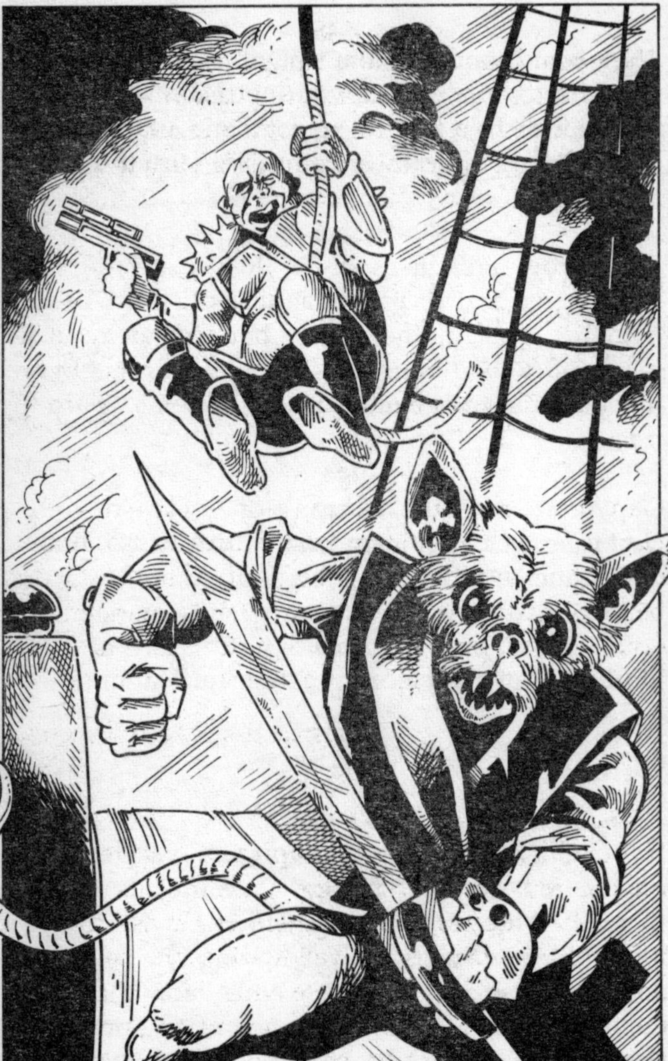

249

The enemy, now at close range, casts a volley of grappling irons into your barge, drawing the two vessels together. The enemy captain, a rodent-faced creature with enormous ears, leads his cut-throats across a gangplank. You must fight.

	SKILL	STAMINA
CAPTAIN BIG-EARS	8	8
POT-BELLIED CUT-THROAT	7	6

If you win, turn to **136**.

250

Glip now turns the red ring one segment anticlockwise. His path is no longer blocked, so, brandishing an electro-lance, he spurs his armoured beast towards you. In response, you manoeuvre your grasshopper and its laser-cannon to face him.

	RATING	LASERS	SHIELDS
GLIP	4	3	8
GRASSHOPPER	–	4	10

If you win, another Glip appears on the vacated spot on the red ring. Scuttlebug, gnashing its fangs, turns the blue ring one segment clockwise, but is foiled. Mutant turns the yellow ring one segment anti-clockwise, and his phase ends. Now the third move begins. Will you rotate the red ring one segment clockwise (turn to **100**), or two segments anti-clockwise (turn to **12**)?

251

Despite your efforts, you are seized by a large Ogre-oid and brought before the Deik. Turn to **51**.

252

Wriggling through the reeds is an exotic, striped thing with a slug's head and torso, two stumpy forearms, leathery flukes and fins. It examines you in a somewhat pernickety manner while menacing you with a multi-barrelled blunderbuss. Eventually it grins toothily. 'So you're a *real*, then! Sorry, but one must be careful nowadays. Oh, for the good old days!' The beast returns your weapons and strikes up a conversation. Apparently it was manufactured by L'Bastin when he first arrived on Aarok. 'Many weird things came out of his tubs in the early days,' the creature reminisces. 'I had good friends among them. We were just part of his grand experiment, of course: small steps towards the discovery of his "perfect" life-form. But I was a failure. He said I was too sensitive, and cared too much for the trees and shrubs. Sambuch the Snail he called me.' It snickers. 'Please, call me Sam!' One day, Sam accidentally overheard a conversation between

L'Bastin and a servant. 'When I heard that I was to be returned to the pot, I decided to escape. So here I am, though not out of trouble yet, I may add.' Sam pauses abruptly, rubs his stalked eyes, then chooses his words carefully. 'You seem a generous soul to me. Perhaps you would be kind enough to help me out of, er, a minor predicament?' Something in his remarks disturbs you. Has he been telling you the truth? If you decide to help him, turn to **144**; otherwise, turn to **218**.

253

You gather up your weapons and free Dr Strangething. You are about to leave the cell when the doctor calls, 'One moment. I know the passage to the surface, but there are traps on the way. No one has ever escaped from these dungeons.' Thinking for a moment, you search Epicurien's body. In a concealed pouch you find a tattered vellum parchment:

(If you wrote down the 'perspex' message earlier, you may now try to translate these runes.) Now, you follow Dr Strangething through the passages. Turn to **316**.

254

However, before you reach Aarok, your communicator crackles with the voice of your leader, King Vaax. 'Another minor change in plans,' he says. 'Within your vicinity is the infamous space pirate, Tungsten-Klaw. He is about to raid a friendly world, and we want you to stop him! That is all!' With a mighty rattle, you re-enter 'real space' in the Adelpha solar system. Your sensors immediately detect Tungsten-Klaw's ship, the *Grand Archipelago*, making its way towards one of the richest planets in the system. Throttling forward, you prepare for battle. Turn to **11**.

255

You touch the correct mechanism, and the sides of the crate disintegrate, revealing its contents: a three-wheeled buggy. It is equipped with two lasers, one on each side, and you observe a large hemispherical hollow on top, probably to sit in. Peculiarly, the laser muzzles each have a small metallic face machined into them; these now eye you suspiciously, and begin chatting to each other! 'What do *you* make of it, Bric?' says the laser on the right. 'Dunno, Brac,' answers the other. 'Wish Head was here. Still, he looks kind o' nervous.' 'Heh, he's got every right to be, I reckon,' replies the right-hand laser. They talk in machine language for a while, then suddenly the buggy rolls forward and swivels to the left: Brac looks menacing. Will you jump to your left (turn to **223**), or to your right (turn to **6**), or dive to the ground (turn to **325**)?

256

You are pushed up against the pillar, and stick fast. The old man cackles, 'By the will of the globe-headed green giant, it must be so!' He turns to move away, but your fourth arm, which is still free, pulls him on to the pillar also. 'We will suffer this fate together then,' you muse ruefully, as both yourself and the screaming old man are slowly covered by dripping goblets of the strange liquid.

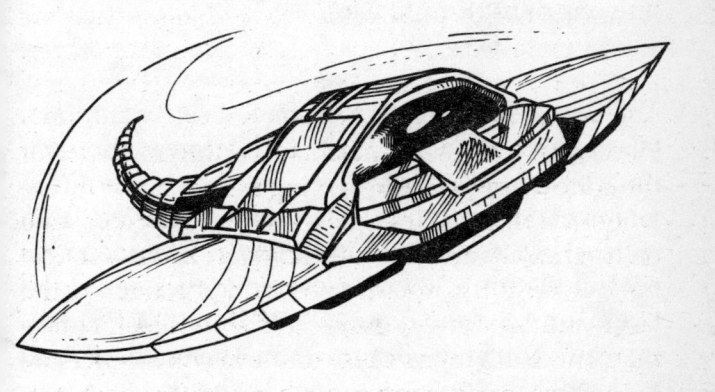

257

Unluckily, as you move along the corridor, your boot connects with a glass spigot that hitherto you had failed to notice, since it was at ankle height. Now the upper end of the spigot cracks and breaks off. From a cavity within it, a long wiry cord unfurls and begins to whip you mercilessly. It is part of the ship's defence network. You may defend yourself only with buckler and electro-javelin, so deduct 1 point from your SKILL temporarily during the combat which follows.

ATTACK WHIP   SKILL 9   TAMINA 4

If you win, the spigot and part of the hoop to which it was attached dissolve, forming an exit on your right. Also, you discover that the left-hand exit further along has become blocked by a newly formed hoop. You may now continue along the long passage (turn to **173**), or pass through the opening on your right (turn to **242**).

258

The game is over and you have been victorious. Giant Jym Ego snorts. 'Bah! You deceived me. You must be a professional player. Still, I am generous to a fault. To the Dome of Marvels you may go.' Jym instructs Marsatu to join you on the Roundabout's central platform. 'Now, close your eyes and don't peek, or I'll send you to the Dome of Horrors instead!' You both obey the giant's instructions, and you sense the rings spinning. Then you feel a waft of air and a heavy jolt. You risk taking a look around. You have indeed reached the Dome of Marvels. In fact, you are sitting on top of it! Turn to **337**.

259

'Do you have any salt?' L'Bastin inquires. 'No? Then we are doomed.' His words ring true, and you die in detention, several weeks later.

260

Operating a scoop, you prepare to pick up an escape module. As you approach, however, an explosive pellet is launched from another starfighter. Its force sends you somersaulting into the module, slicing it in half. Reduce your SHIELDS by 2 points *permanently*, and deduct 2 points from your STAMINA. Recovering, will you proceed towards the Valioog mothership at speed (turn to 369), perform an 'Eigenvector Roll' to attack another starfighter from the rear (turn to 320), launch an atomic flare (turn to 143), or perform a complex turn (turn to 389)?

261

For most of the day you track the droid through the woodlands, across tiny brooks and along rocky gulleys. Quite obviously he is familiar with the region. Curiously, although he is aware of your presence (his three faces give him all-round vision), he makes no attempt to conceal himself. But when dusk approaches, the droid leaves the forest and vanishes behind a bluff of blue moonstone. When you follow, you cannot see him. Your only clue is a faint trail which forks left towards a spiny ridge; and right, towards a steep incline. Will you follow the left path (turn to 354), or the right path (turn to 307), or continue trailing the base of the bluff (turn to 375)?

262

You leap into a tube-car filled with dignitaries. Menacing them with your laser, you steer the craft along the tube and enter the city. At the first station you reach, you leap from the vehicle and, sealing its doors with your laser, follow along a broad triangular passage. Turn to 323.

263

Before you make your getaway, a dozen more spiders show up. After a fierce struggle, in the course of which you knock several spiders unconscious and plant your boot squarely in the face of another, you are overwhelmed, tied up and beaten. Deduct 2 points from your STAMINA. You are dragged for miles across the desert towards the spiders' camp, arriving there at first light. Turn to 327.

264

You spin half starboard and move away, then spin full to port to face the Deik's flank. But his electrode whips your craft. Deduct 2 points from your STAMINA. If you have a dart-gun, turn to 398; otherwise, will you press a red button (turn to 109), or pull on a wire (turn to 314)?

265

The bowl you are standing in starts to fill with fire. Roll as many dice as you have titanium cubes. If the total of your roll equals

1, 2, 3, 4 or 5	Deduct 5 points from your STAMINA
6, 7	Deduct 4 points from your STAMINA
8, 9	Deduct 3 points from your STAMINA
10, 11	Deduct 2 points from your STAMINA
12	Deduct 1 point from your STAMINA

The bowl then empties of fire. If you are still alive, you may pass through the bowl and follow the tunnel on the other side. Turn to **200**.

266

With a squelch, you run the jellified creature over, then reverse the scooter through the swinging doors, into a vast chamber. Within, tall trees grow on large pontoons: whole groves of oranges, lemons, peaches and other fruits. You have entered the space station's hydroponic gardens where all the fresh food is produced. Luckily, the bruised blob has not followed you; you dismount and examine the gardens at leisure. Will you turn your nose towards a run of strawberries (turn to **362**), or try an unrecognizable, sweet-smelling fruit (turn to **197**)?

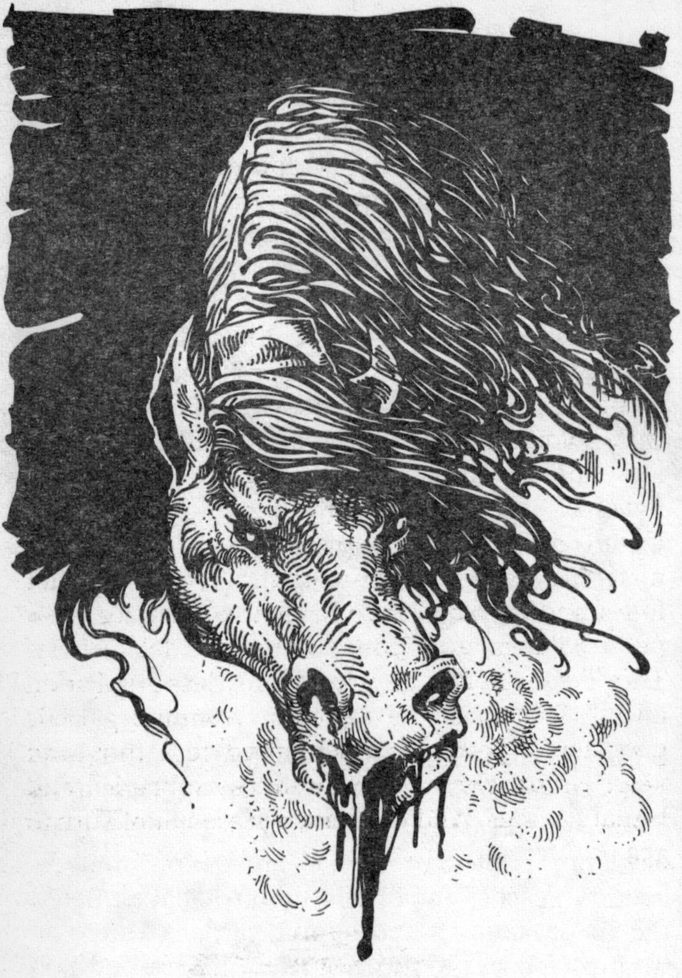

267

Passing a large tablet printed with incomprehensible letters of red and yellow, you enter what you believe to be a small shrine. Within, on a low brass pedestal, is an obsidian sculpture, six feet high, fashioned like a raindrop. The front of the 'shrine' is open to view from the causeway and so, as the lantern-bearing figure approaches, you leap behind the sculpture, pressing yourself against it. This action is disastrous! As you touch the stone, it liquefies and splashes to the floor like cold water. In its place, standing upon the pedestal, is a hideous ruby-coloured creature with a horse-like head, two legs and no arms. It is wrapped in light-grey pyjamas embellished with darker-grey arrows. Upon its head is a floppy peaked cap of similar material. Leering at you it rants: 'Free! Free after four hundred years. Such harsh treatment for a few petty killings and some harmless debauchery! They'll rue the day they locked fearless Fog Farkin away!' You recall the name: a tyrannical galactic gangster of yesteryear, sentenced to a thousand years' imprisonment for countless robberies and brutal slayings. And you have released him! Turn to **359**.

268

Farkin's sticky tongue releases you. Gasping for breath, you turn on your laser-sword and attack the evil gangster.

FOG FARKIN   SKILL 9   STAMINA 6

If you win, turn to 294.

269

Your ship is pierced by a huge tungsten bolt, which destroys a laser pod. Reduce both your SHIELDS and your LASERS by 1 point *permanently*.

Starspray: Pitch +21.5 . . . Roll +112 . . .
   Yaw +1.5 . . .
Enemy: Pitch +35 . . . Roll +60 . . .
   Yaw +13 . . .
Relative speed 2000 . . .

Now you may:

Halve speed, roll +90	Turn to 34
Halve speed, pitch +60, roll +30	Turn to 22
Maintain speed, pitch −15, roll +60, yaw +5	Turn to 217

270

'Splendid!' Zud exclaims. 'This is what I have in mind: not far from here is a drinking tavern, frequented by many of the brigands, wayliffs and unscrupulous profiteers who infest this planet. Within the tavern, adorning its walls and spaces, you will see many wondrous curios which belong to the tavern's owner: an old purple Deik. I am particularly interested in one of the objects he possesses. It is an enormous brain of a Bulb-Headed Bicephalon of Atranda-Red, the most intelligent creatures in the known multiverses. The brain has been perfectly preserved in a crystal decanter. I need the brain, in good condition, to power my craft, and since the miserable old Deik refuses to part with it, you will steal it for me!' Surely Zud must be mad! Will you draw your laser pistol and threaten Zud (turn to **162**) or obey his request (turn to **315**)?

271

You follow a coloured stream for several hours, until its course slows at the entrance of a broad lake. Upon the lake, resting on massive piers, is a huge crystalline spaceship, bristling with weapons. A high causeway curls away from it to the lake's edge. If you have previously met Schaine the Delphon sprite, turn to **171**. Otherwise, you may wish to enter the ship via the causeway (turn to **317**), or vacate the area, following a trail away from the causeway (turn to **354**).

272

Just as you dispatch the second Brute, more outlandish creatures appear at the doorway. One six-armed critter, with a baton in one hand and a net in another, snares you and beats you senseless. Deduct 2 points from your STAMINA. You are dragged, bleeding, into the house, and left in a room alone for a while. Eventually, the six-armed thing returns: 'Boss and Woderwick will see you now,' it grunts. 'Better be on your best behaviour, if you know what's good for you!' Turn to 367.

273

The remaining spiders, scuttling to the tops of nearby columns, shriek at you and begin spinning long webs. The nearest spider streams a cord across the gap. It glues fast, allowing three other spiders to rush across at you. Will you kick the spiders (turn to 210), or turn your pistol on them (turn to 228)?

274

You enter a long thin gallery. Violet windows, sweeping the entire length of the hall, give you a grand view of your spaceship, still moored against the air-tube. Suddenly, you become aware of a hungry orange blob which is rolling towards you. As blobs are notoriously difficult to kill, you decide to flee to the opposite end of the hall. On the way, your shoulder brushes against an object; it is a human skeleton, one of the blob's former victims. The twisted finger-bones still clutch a couple of items, and a plastic pouch lying on the floor contains a few more. You just have time to scoop up two of the following items:

> flare pistol
> chain
> compressed-air canister
> wrist-watch
> club
> chewing gum

When you have decided which two objects you collect, add them to your *Adventure Sheet*, then turn to 332.

275

Marsatu leaps behind you as the Prefecta attacks.

PREFECTA   SKILL 8   STAMINA 8

If you win, turn to 24.

276

You take the air-tube to Vault 7 and pass through a triangular opening to enter L'Bastin's laboratory. It is a large rectangular chamber with a gaudy tangerine ceiling and sickly brown walls. Lining many of the walls are aluminium racks crammed with colourful bottles, smoking flasks, corked cylinders and tubes. A pungent odour rises from thick dust and spilt liquids carpeting the floor – certainly L'Bastin had been a most untidy scientist! In the main, however, your attention is drawn to the opposite end of the room, beyond dozens of rows of high wooden benches, to a point where three dog-like beings are shovelling powdered chemicals into a mechanical hopper. Stealing closer, you examine them in detail. By their outlandish dress and their queer manner of speech, you recognize them as Yappies, a race of intelligent canines from Quadranx-Mauve. Apparently they are laboratory assistants, preparing the chemical mix for the second batch of Prefectas. 'Zap, my man, Brag,' says the one wearing the bowler hat, blue reflectors and satin pantaloons, 'it's freezo time. Clear yar pads, it's time for a gulp of rocket cola.' Zap and Brag down tools and follow the other into a side room where, after a noisy gurgle, they can be heard giggling and quietly humming weird tunes. When all seems safe, you sneak up to the gyrating hopper and crumble your rock-salt into the mix. But as you turn aside, the now tipsy Yappies return. 'Hey, hey!' says one. 'What's this – a snoop? I'm jabbin' m' blabber to those Prefecta dudes, or m' bonnet'll roll!' They all turn to leave the laboratory. If you have the sphere containing the audio-amplifying headset, turn to **132**; otherwise, turn to **115**.

277

'Ya' flim-flam, scint not!' snaps the old man angrily. 'You're for orange pot, ha!' He staggers over to the gong, sounds it twice, and points towards you. He has awakened the Deik! Turn to **51**.

278

All the square-shaped tiles change colour: orange to green, green to blue, blue to orange. Will you step on tile B2 (turn to **327**), or tile C3 (turn to **129**)?

279

Eventually, you reach Aarok and exit from the warp. However, as you manoeuvre the *Starspray* through the atmosphere's defences of mines, projectiles and atomic blimps, you are detected and attacked by an automated defence module.

DEFENCE
 MODULE   RATING 6   LASERS 2   SHIELDS 6

If you win, turn to **52**.

280

Unluckily for you, the Prefecta's scooter is clogged with thick mud and will not start. With the other spider-craft approaching, you decide to climb on to the tree branch, and take aim at it. Turn to **165**.

281

Before you can climb to the top, a dozen hairy spider-critters leap over a dune, shrieking wildly. Three of them begin to climb your pillar; the others scuttle up nearby columns. Will you plant your heel in the face of the first spider below you (turn to **210**), shoot several off a nearby pillar (turn to **228**), or use your laser-sword and buckler to dislodge those below (turn to **178**)?

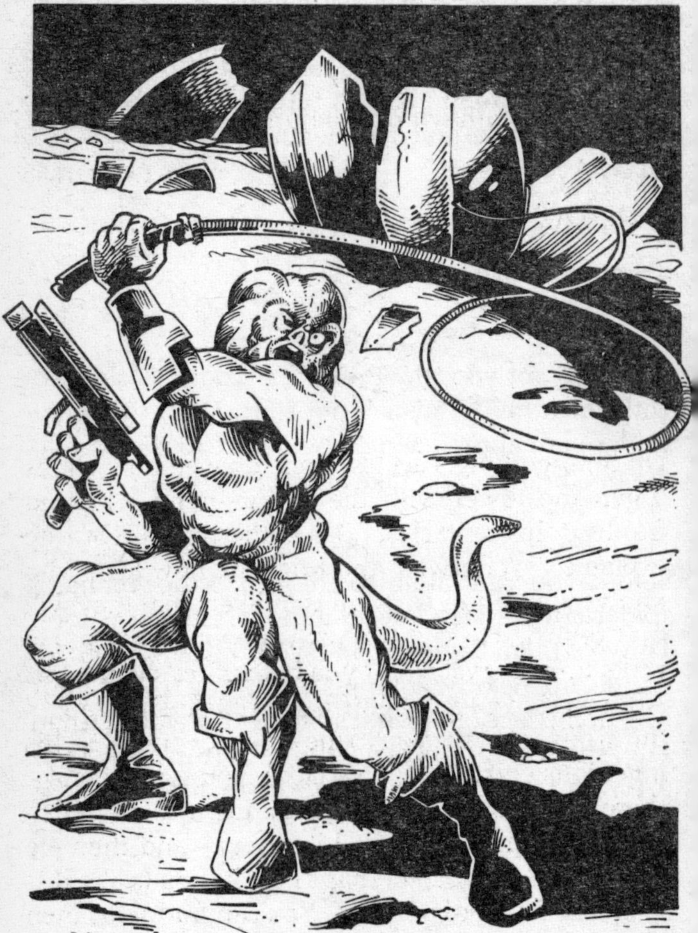

282

The enemy ship, passing close overhead, drops a metal sphere to the desert floor before continuing to pursue Long-nose's barge. The sphere bursts open to reveal a savage, apricot-coloured mutantoid. It attacks you with whip and thunder-gun.

MUTANTOID   SKILL 8   STAMINA 6

If you win, turn to 32.

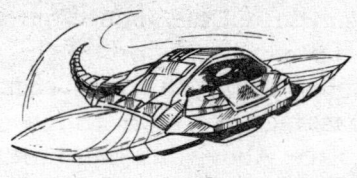

283

Dr Strangething cackles from above, and slides down the tower with the minute-hand wrapped firmly in his tentacles. '*This* is the real cursor,' he explains. 'Woderwick and Kogo are now lost, who knows where and when. It is unlikely that they will ever return.' He says this with knowing finality. He picks up the crystal and you both enter the manor. After a rest and a delightful cup of tea, Dr Strangething offers to take you to the defence centre, via his ingenious crystal. 'Not too close, you understand – there are sensors and defences down there which will detect the crystal and its users – and then we would be in trouble! Perhaps I'll take you to Vault 5, near the Dome of Marvels. You can find your own way from there.' He laughs; the crystal expands, the cursor is directed and you are transported. Turn to 2.

284

You eventually find your way to the main entrance of the mansion and out on to the terraces surrounding it. Not far away stand Marsatu and Bok. Marsatu appears to be giving the servant some instructions – what a pity you cannot lip-read! After a minute Marsatu turns to you, while Bok, having received a pat from his master, trots away north-eastwards along the causeway. 'Hm,' begins Marsatu, 'last night you began to tell me about your mission.' (This you do not recall.) 'Well, I'll help you right enough; just follow me.' You are led back through the manor's passages to a room with a huge old-fashioned fireplace. Above this, on a broad mantelpiece, is a pewter figurine to which Marsatu now draws your attention. 'Behold!' he cries, twisting a curiously wrought golden key into the figurine's single eye-socket. The entire fireplace swivels aside to reveal, upon a recessed shelf behind, seven small crystalline globes. Each sphere is transparent, and contains a tiny object. 'Choose two,' says Marsatu. You may choose any two from the following list and add them to your *Adventure Sheet*. The spheres contain:

> a drill-helmet
> some battle-armour
> an infra-red sensor helmet
> an audio-amplifying headset
> jet boots
> a metal hound
> power-gauntlets

When you have chosen, turn to **233**.

285

You take some minor damage from bubble-bomb splinters. Deduct 1 point from your STAMINA.

Starspray: Pitch +19 ... Roll +82 ... Yaw −18 ...
Enemy: Pitch +35 ... Roll +60 ... Yaw +13 ...
Relative speed 2000 ...

You may:

Maintain speed, yaw −6.5	Turn to **148**
Maintain speed, pitch +15, yaw −31	Turn to **177**
Halve speed, roll +105, yaw −5	Turn to **203**

286

The enemy barge fires a small missile, which impacts near you on the iron-clad deck. Deduct 2 points from your STAMINA. Turn to **249**.

287

Shooting is ineffective, as the bolts bounce off the Brutes' armour. One Brute says to the other: 'Hey, Marigold, looks like our lucky day. What a bunny we have here!' 'Yeah, Nob,' says Marigold gruffly. 'Let's hit him with the clubbers.' You scramble to your feet to escape the flailing clubs, and draw your laser-sword.

	SKILL	STAMINA
NOB	8	12
MARIGOLD	6	12

If you win, turn to **166**; if you lose, turn to **116**.

288

Alas, the hound is defective, and turns on you, gnashing its fangs. Marsatu and the Prefecta almost split their sides with laughter. 'Heel!' you scream. 'Heel!'

METAL HOUND   SKILL 9   STAMINA 3

If you win, turn to 275.

289

An enormous nose appears over the side of the barge, accompanied by a small, bug-eyed face. 'Ahoy there, stranger!' yells this creature, the captain. 'I'm short on crew; if you'll climb aboard, I'm sure we could come to some arrangement.' Wishing to put some distance between yourself and the desert spiders, you climb the rope ladder and enter the barge. Turn to 364.

290

Before you submerge, there is a loud explosion and the bell's top hatch is ripped off. Deduct 2 points from your STAMINA. Three ferocious Prefectas scramble through the hole and attack.

	SKILL	STAMINA
SNAPPY SERGEANT PREFECTA	8	8
CRAFTY CORPORAL PREFECTA	8	6
PUGNACIOUS PRIVATE PREFECTA	8	7

If you win, will you prefer to divert the craft towards the north-west (turn to **128**), or order the computer to change to action plan number 358 (turn to **358**), or number 368 (turn to **368**)?

291

Your ship begins to spin backwards; your electrode-probe whirls violently and comes into contact with your own sphere. Deduct 2 points from your STAMINA. The Deik appears to starboard. Soon he will be within range. Will you:

Blow in a red tube?	Turn to **234**
Twist a triangular knob?	Turn to **26**
Pull an iron ring on the floor?	Turn to **47**

292

In an attempt to avoid enemy flak, you accelerate the *Starspray's* engines way beyond their safe operating range, and force the craft through a tight turn. The energy banks overload dangerously and you burn out a magno-seal. Turn to **389**.

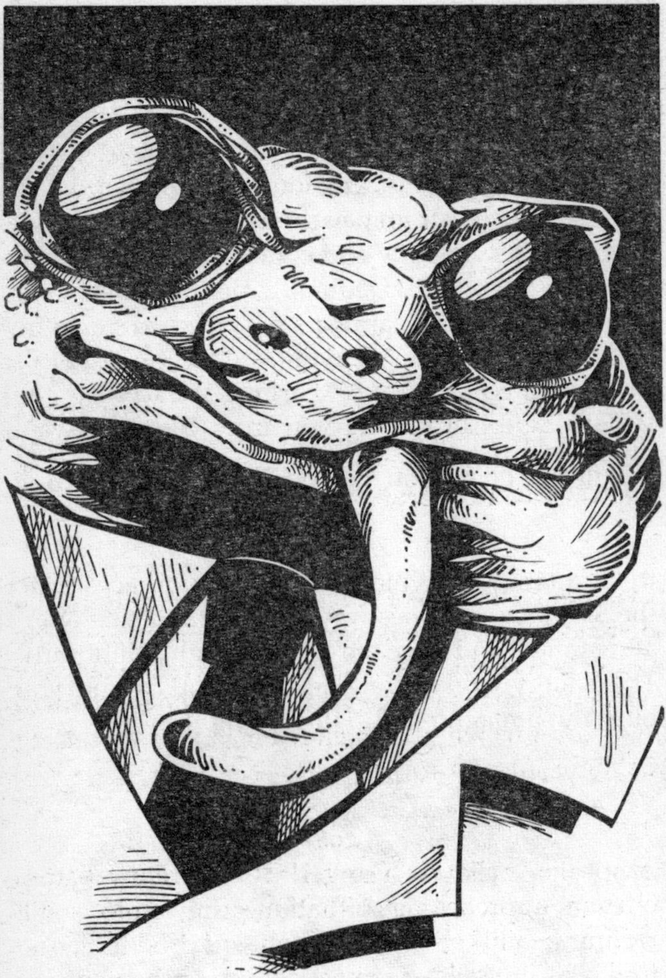

293

Now the toad-faced creature appears behind you. 'Right, that's mine. My heirloom!' he says, greedily eyeing the spectron projector and its bag of explosive pellets. But a spectron projector may be very useful to you on your mission. Will you hand it to him (turn to 88), or do you prefer to keep it yourself (turn to 381)?

294

You search Fog's body and find a steel file. (Add this to your *Adventure Sheet*.) Turning, you notice the lantern-figure observing you from the causeway. He had been watching your life-and-death tussle without once offering assistance! Turn to 349.

295

Eventually the noise fades to a faint tinkle in the distance, then there is silence. After you spend the night in a fitful doze, morning arrives. You may wish to leave the village via Spitflak's Street (turn to 160), or further investigate the buildings during daylight (turn to 380).

296

A speaker bellows: 'Danger! Three enemy battle-cruisers approaching. Situation grim!' Rhio is still reclining in his chair and, when you prod him, you find that he is dead; obviously the excitement *had* been too much for him! The speaker continues: 'Situation desperate! Suggest you pursue action plan number 208, 358 or 368 . . . input required . . .'

297–298

The auto-control is awaiting your response. Without knowing what the action plan numbers entail, will you pursue plan number 208 (turn to **208**), 358 (turn to **358**), or 368 (turn to **368**)?

297
The blob soon catches and devours you.

298
Only after a fierce struggle do you manage to repulse the spiders. Those still alive retreat a short distance away and spend the entire night nursing their wounds in a hollow near by. At dawn, as you are squatting miserably on top of the pillar wondering how to escape, you detect a faint humming. In the distance you perceive a large, flat air-barge skimming towards you, its distinctive red-and-white pennant fluttering in the breeze. Soon the barge is hovering only twenty feet overhead, dropping a rope ladder to you as it sends the spiders scuttling from the path of a heat-ray. You have been saved! Turn to **289**.

299

The Glip turns the red ring one segment anti-clockwise, but cannot attack. However, when Scuttlebug rotates the blue ring one segment clockwise, he has a clear path and attacks your flank.

	RATING	LASERS	SHIELDS
SCUTTLEBUG	5	2	12
GRASSHOPPER	–	3	10

If you win, turn to **258**.

300

With a most peculiar sensation, your laser-sword's pommel enters his head with a squelch. 'Barty' flops to the ground and transforms into his true self: a bright orange jelly! Before your astonished eyes it melts through the overalls and re-forms into an angry blob. It is a Valcretian Surprise, a monster capable of flexing itself into almost any shape. You were to be this one's next dinner! The blob now rolls towards you, blocking your exit to the escape hatch and melting the air-seal shut. Will you run down a bend in the corridor (turn to **60**), or will you dive through a narrow metal chute on your right (turn to **242**)?

301

You pay for the use of a pit – which is actually a hollow in the floor, several feet in diameter. (Deduct 2 credits from your *Adventure Sheet*.) As you sit there, a tall green steward fills the pit to the brim with a dark liquid, then offers you a straw, before departing. Now, sipping at the vile concoction, you wonder how you will accomplish Zud's task; you are also mindful of Gnasha, chewing away merrily inside you. Your thoughts are soon interrupted by a drunken old man from the next pit. His bowl is empty, and he punches you in the arm and declares: 'I'm short on lack-knee – ya' not!' Unsure of the correct reply, will you answer:

'Tush, move ya' lack-knee on all!'?	Turn to **334**
'Aye, short o' lack-knee ya' not!'?	Turn to **191**
'Tush ya' lack-knee jarg', try ni'er bowl!'?	Turn to **277**

302

You do not swim very far before a large, toothy Gooblepotomus pokes its snout out of the water. 'Ah, mmm . . .' it burbles, 'it must be time for a little snack!' As you find it difficult to defend yourself in water, deduct 2 points from your SKILL temporarily during the following combat.

GOOBLEPOTOMUS   SKILL 6   STAMINA 10

If you win, you had better swim back to shore before you find yourself being attacked by another unwholesome creature. You may either set out after the droid (turn to 261), or travel up the vale to locate a village and help (turn to 344).

303

The Glip turns the red ring one segment anti-clockwise, and charges on his beast towards you.

	RATING	LASERS	SHIELDS
GLIP	4	3	8
GRASSHOPPER	–	4	10

If you win, then it is Scuttlebug's phase. He decides not to rotate the blue ring. Turn to 212.

304

Suddenly the robot's arms are activated. One of these grips your hand and shakes it so vigorously that your arm is torn off! Deduct 4 points from your STAMINA and 1 point from your SKILL. 'Oops, sorry!' says the robot. 'Thought you were a machine, too. Here, let me help.' It produces a flesh-mastic spray; this, coating your injured joint, stops the bleeding in seconds (if you are still alive). Then, just as amazingly, the robot hurls your limp arm away. 'That's useless now,' it declares, 'but try this one: it's *much* better, really.' This time, it pulls out a horrible, rubbery tentacle, which it forces on to your joint and glues in place! The robot, quite satisfied with the result, deactivates itself. You soon discover that, in fact, the tentacle is easy to manage and in many instances would prove more useful than a humanoid arm. Still . . . Eventually you recover from the shock. Will you examine the small hemisphere, if you have not already done so (turn to 149), or the unmarked crate (turn to 255); or do you prefer to return to the sleeping Rhio, in the level above (turn to 296)?

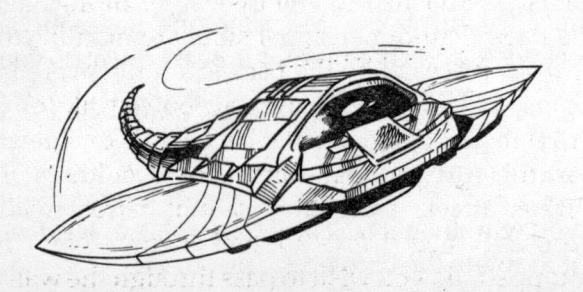

305

The entire bookshelf revolves, carrying you with it into a dimly lit storeroom which is cluttered with gadgetry. Unable to find a way back to the study, and unable to find another exit from the room, you decide to spend some time prying around. The significance of your find now becomes apparent. The store contains a huge cache of weapons: laser-rifles, rays, vacuum grenades, battle armour and much, much more – enough to equip a small, élite army. You even find a dozen suits of fully charged Newbury's pan-dimensional polyarmour, an extremely sophisticated item which enables its wearer to exist in both the 3rd and the 17th dimension simultaneously. The practical result of this miracle technology is that, for a time, the user may pass through walls and other obstacles without damaging either himself, the suit or the obstacle. You have never worn pan-dimensional armour before, but decide to try on a suit now. First you don the moulded face-mask, then the front plate, with its lasers mounted in a small chest cavity, then the thigh pads, greaves and, finally, gloves. These items are attached to you by leather thongs tied at the back. Pan-dimensional suits are manufactured as front-pieces only; the back is left uncovered and exposed. Thus the wearer can only walk forward through an obstacle, never backwards or sideways. For this reason, pan-dimensional soldiers must always attack, since they cannot retreat without exposing their backs to the enemy. Now fully equipped, do you wish to pass through the wall and back into the study (turn to **385**), or slip through the floor to investigate the basement (turn to **184**)?

306

You respond jubilantly, 'I have some salt, but how can I administer it? We are still caged in, after all.' 'Not for long,' says L'Bastin, plunging one arm into the posidon tank. With a yank, he pulls loose the rubber mouth-piece and hose. 'Here, wrap this round one of your hands,' he tells you. When you have done so, he points to the bars where Marsatu was killed. 'Observe: those bars are quite dull, and covered with soot: a good insulator. Their power has been much reduced. Now, clench those bars with the rubber hose, and bend them outwards.' Apprehensively, you touch the bars and bend them out of shape, receiving only minor shocks as you do so. Deduct 2 points from your STAMINA. Stepping gingerly through the gap, you turn to help L'Bastin out; at this moment, the warder returns. 'Caught you in the act!' he shouts, levelling his needle-gun. In a flash you leap on him, wrestling for the weapon.

WARDER   SKILL 8   STAMINA 8

If you win, turn to **356**.

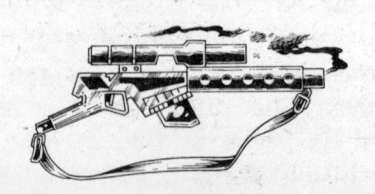

307

You follow the path along the edge of a deep chasm, then down a narrow gulch towards a purple-and-orange river. Foolishly, you decide to wade across the stream before testing it: it is caustic and burns your skin. Deduct 2 points from your STAMINA. When you have crossed, you rest on the bank for a while, wrapping your wounds in broad leaves picked from a nearby ointbush, a plant with extraordinary healing properties. You also stow away several more leaves for future use. (Add them to your *Adventure Sheet*.) Turn to **271**.

308

You just avoid falling against one of the sticky pillars. The old man raises his staff, declaring, 'By the will of the globe-headed green giant, you must suffer the great ignominy!' He attacks again, prodding with his staff.

OLD MAN   SKILL 8   STAMINA 4

If you win, turn to **30**.

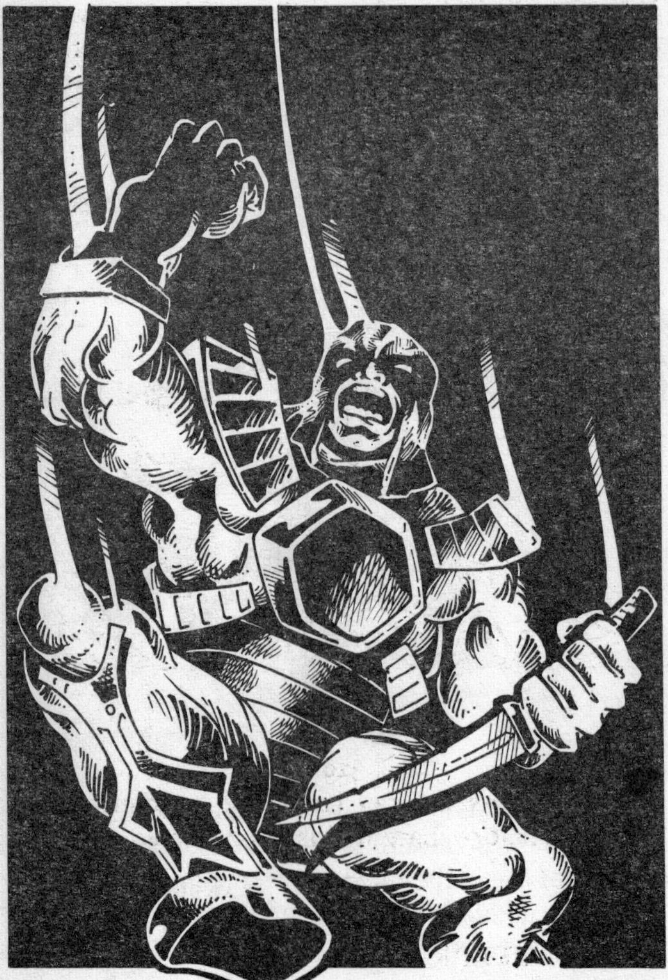

309

You decide to hide in the ventilator shaft but, within it, you are suddenly confronted by a red-hooded humanoid who attacks you with a long, curved knife.

RED-HOODED
　TERRORIST　　　SKILL 7　　　STAMINA 8

If you win, turn to **78**.

310

The Glip turns the red circle one segment anti-clockwise before charging his steed into your flank.

	RATING	LASERS	SHIELDS
GLIP	4	3	8
GRASSHOPPER	–	3	10

If you win, then it is Scuttlebug's phase. He elects not to turn the blue ring at all. Turn to **212**.

311

Presently, you close upon the planet: a majestic world of reds and greens, patched with swirling white clouds. Grazing the atmosphere, your craft begins to heat up; it is not long before the space-weed, burnt to fine ash, produces a trailing, fiery wake behind the *Starspray*. But when you turn away from the planet towards space, your hull is suddenly pierced by a lightning bolt, surging from a cloud below. The cabin pressure drops rapidly; as you fight to maintain control, a fire breaks out in an aft storage pod. Booster power fails, and your ship plummets towards a ridge of scarlet hills; a crash-landing is imminent. Switching to manual glide, you steer yourself between two rocky pinnacles into a long, narrow valley. Looming ahead is a dark lake, surrounded by trees and a bank of grey shingles. Will you try to land on the lake (turn to 44), or on the bank of shingles (turn to 96)?

312

You are stunned by a gravity-bomb which detonates near by. Reduce your SHIELDS by 1 point *permanently*.

Starspray: Pitch +44 ... Roll +202 ... Yaw +21 ...
Enemy: Pitch +35 ... Roll +60 ... Yaw +13 ...
Relative speed 500 ...

Will you:

Accelerate to 1000, maintain course?   Turn to **22**
Accelerate to 2000, pitch +40, roll
  +120, yaw +26?   Turn to **269**
Maintain speed, pitch +30, yaw
  +30?   Turn to **347**

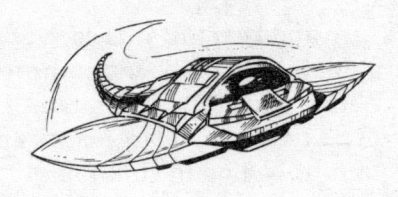

313

You rest in your spaceship until evening, while Krill amasses his force: several hundred strong and equipped with a variety of weapons, including lasers, pulsers, blasters, blazers, flame-lances and vacuum grenades. Under colourful banners they march across the plains and over a roll of hills, towards the enemy ship on Lake Droog. Several hours later, the sky in that direction flashes with orange and red; the attack has begun! Eventually, your ear-twinge throbs to the sound of Krill's voice. 'They're taking off. Now – attack!' Simultaneously you see, rising above the hills, a monstrous crystalline spaceship, bristling with laser-cannon. You take off and swoop into range.

DELPHON BATTLESHIP
                    RATING 5   LASERS 5   SHIELDS 8

If you win, turn to **328**.

314

The spheres turn and bear towards each other. Both spheres manipulate their grabbers; both are blocked by shields. With a thud, the ships ram. Deduct 1 point from your STAMINA. A large crack appears in your sphere and it begins to sink rapidly. Time is running out. Will you:

Do nothing?	Turn to 291
Whistle through a mouthpiece?	Turn to 109
Bite a blue chew-bulb?	Turn to 338
Scream loudly?	Turn to 47

315

Zud leads you towards the tavern: a slime-green apartment with a large sign on the wall outside reading: 'DEAD FETHP INN – LIZARDOIDS AND MUTANTS KEEP OUT!' When Zud departs to his chambers, you enter the inn. Turn to 83.

316

You enter a bowl-shaped chamber with an exit at the far side. As you enter, a voice speaks, 'Roll the titanium cubes to pass.' If you have any titanium cubes, turn to **265**; otherwise, turn to **152**.

317

Your path is blocked by two Mutants, with clawed arms extending from their faces and legs. 'Too much muscle, not enough fat on that one,' growls one to the other. 'Yeah,' comes the reply, 'but he'll taste just fine after a good roastin'.' They attack you with flame-lances and iron prongs.

	SKILL	STAMINA
DROOLING MUTANT	8	8
CLUMSY MUTANT	5	10

If you win, you decide to retreat from the causeway, preferring to follow the path towards a series of low hills. Turn to **354**.

318

You press on for miles, passing beneath arches of streaked marble and swirling agate, beyond houses, shrines and conservatories, silent for over three hundred years. The Dome of Marvels is still several leagues to your west when the lanterns' hues change to maroon, cobalt and tired grey. High above, the first of many tiny lamp-lights flicker and sparkle into life – specks of brilliant white and gold, shining like stars. It is evening. At this time you see, a mile or so ahead, the glow of a small, hand-held lantern swaying gently back and forth. Its owner, a tall, lean, sinister figure, appears to be swaggering slowly towards you. Will you await his arrival (turn to **349**), or, hiding in a nearby shrine, allow him to pass (turn to **267**)?

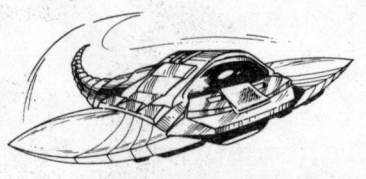

319

The droid's master is Krill Babbit, a humanoid with tanned grey skin and a large round nose supporting a drooping moustache – he looks like a walrus! Still, he is a pleasant enough sort. 'Yes, I am the master of this droid, these caves,' he snorts, 'and, once, this entire planet. That was until Schaine, a war-sprite from Delphon, arrived in her huge sky-ship, several years ago.' If you have already encountered Schaine the Delphon sprite, turn to **236**; otherwise, turn to **341**.

320

Luckily, you perform the roll just in time, as a spike-fighter was about to ram you. Now, wheeling around your new enemy's fuselage, you release a searing laser-bolt.

VALIOOG SPIKE-
 FIGHTER   RATING 4 LASERS 3 SHIELDS 4

If you win, will you launch a lightning ball (turn to **143**), approach the Valioog mothership (turn to **369**), perform a victory roll (turn to **389**), or scan the enemy ship electrically (turn to **215**)?

321

All the circles now change colour: orange to green, green to blue, blue to orange. Will you step on tile C3 (turn to **177**), or tile D4 (turn to **396**)?

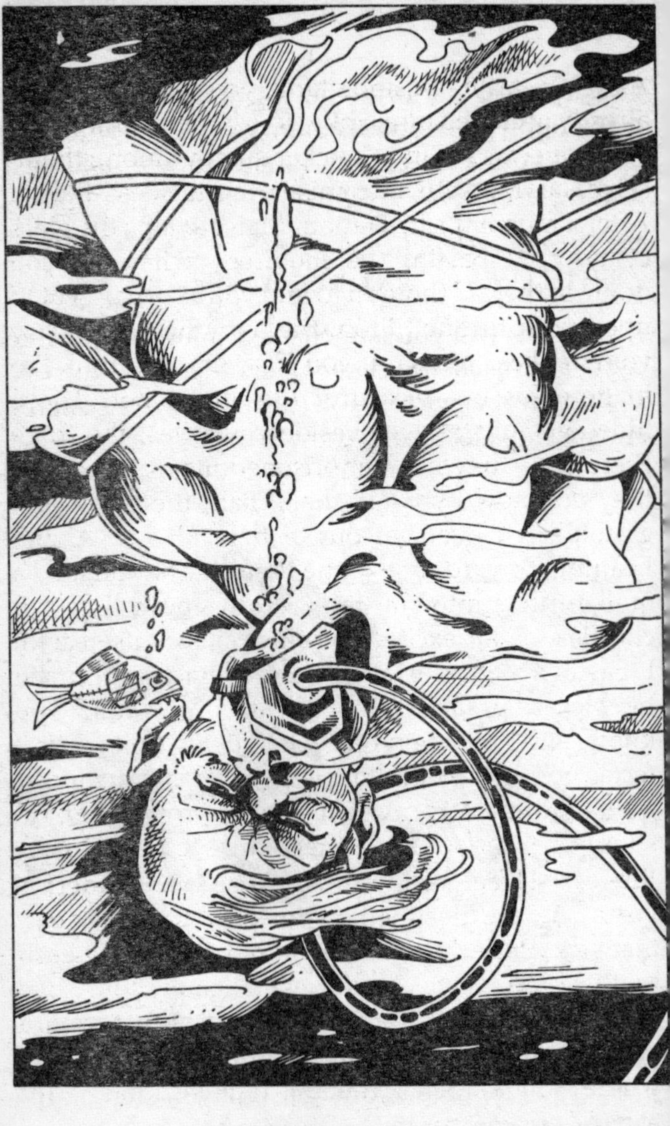

As you near the posidon tank, you realize that it is already occupied by a lanky, four-armed humanoid. The Prefectas begin to snicker quietly among themselves as Marsatu recognizes the luckless figure. After a moment's hesitation, Marsatu taps the glass cylinder. 'L'Bastin,' he inquires, 'what are you doing in there? I thought to find you as usual, seated upon your throne.' From the ivory horn, a dreary voice replies: 'Marsatu, you *idiot*! Do you think I'm in here for my pleasure? Of course not! Those hideous monstrosities beside you – yes, the three Prefectas – they have imprisoned me in here. Yes, they do know I created them! Bah, they're so ungrateful! If I ever get out of here I'll . . . Aagh!' Leaning forward, one of the Prefectas has pushed a quill further into the tank. 'Now, now, L.B.,' it chortles, as an excited tinselfish busies itself with L'Bastin's left earlobe, 'you demean yourself by bickering, and your threats don't suit. You know, and soon everyone will find out, that we Prefectas will tolerate nothing less than being treated as lords and masters. And it is only proper that we should be, for we are perfect, are we not? Perfect life-forms! I feel wonderful, because I *am* wonderful! We alone are destined to rule the galaxy.' With that, the Prefecta launches into a lengthy speech that would have made even giant Jym Ego feel subservient. When it finishes, both Marsatu and yourself are dragged away to a prison cage, where you await a gruelling interrogation. Turn to **225**.

323

After a while, you locate a signboard.

'LOCATION: RED DOG CENTRAL . . . VAULT 1 . . . BUILDING 13'

it reads, and below this:

'RESTRICTED AREA AHEAD. DANGER!'

Boldly, you follow a wide corridor into this area, passing numerous side-passages before arriving at a large, closed air-hatch. Projecting from the hatch are two handles, one with a round, red pommel, the other with a square, blue pommel. You recall that you must reach the defence centre in Vault 6 in the Dome of Marvels, and that the hatch before you probably leads to Vault 2. Will you:

Turn the red and blue handles clockwise?	Turn to 93
Turn red clockwise, blue anti-clockwise?	Turn to 386
Turn red and blue anti-clockwise?	Turn to 118
Turn red anti-clockwise, blue clockwise?	Turn to 192

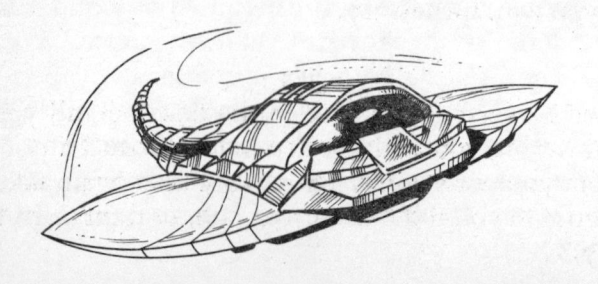

324

You slowly wash the green slime from the creature. Unluckily, you also uncover two other beasts, which had been stuck for some time, and are now quite hungry.

	SKILL	STAMINA
DUCK-BILL CATERPILLAR	8	6
ANGRY YELLOW BLOB	6	6

If you win, turn to **387**.

325

Brac's laser burns a hole in the floor behind you, showering you with molten metal. Deduct 1 point from your STAMINA. The deadly laser again takes aim. Will you roll left (turn to **158**), or right (turn to **247**)?

326

You soon get lost in the manor's complex labyrinth of corridors, stairways and twisting tunnels. Exasperated, you open one of the few doors you come to and enter a spacious chamber. All the walls are lined with shelves, and all the shelves are filled with books, three-dimensional photographs, and mysterious knick-knacks. You are in a private study. Curiously for some reason, three books on one shelf have been placed upside down. Will you take down:

Relative Non-Relativity?	Turn to **104**
Poets of the 57th Century?	Turn to **355**
Baba's Book of Homemade Wines?	Turn to **305**

327

Bound and beaten, you are brought before the chief spider, Queen Slin. 'Well, well,' she babbles, 'this one's so juicy and tender, and plenty of meat on them bones. Not at all like most I receive. We'll hang you up for several days, mind, just to let you stew a bit. Then it's yum yummy!' On her orders you are taken away and strung up in a thick cocoon, dangling between two desert trees. To either side of you are many other cocoons containing a variety of creatures, big and small, but all quite lifeless. Not far away, a solitary spider-guard is curiously examining the weapons recently taken from you. The other spiders have crawled into their underground nests to escape from the desert heat. Roll one die. If you roll 1, 2 or 3, turn to **374**; if you roll 4 or 5, turn to **391**; if you roll a 6, turn to **230**.

328

The Delphon ship wobbles and jerks, then explodes above the lake. Through the ear-twinge, you hear Krill exclaim delightedly, 'Well done! You have destroyed the evil Schaine in her ship. We wish you good fortune in your journey ahead. Farewell!' You perform an elaborate victory-roll before rocketing back into space. But immediately, you pick up a weak distress signal on your radio, from some distance ahead. Will you go to help (turn to **137**), or enter a light-warp to continue to Aarok (turn to **182**)?

329

In order to increase speed, Captain Long-nose orders you overboard, to lighten his barge. Climbing down a long rope, you reach the desert dunes and watch the barge float away towards the city. Turn to **282**.

330

'Very well, I'll have them. Yes, they look quite juicy.' Gnasha chews through all your bonds, then looks at you. 'I'm still hungry, and metal isn't all I eat!' It licks its chops. 'Oh, no you don't,' you reply, and kick it across the floor. It rebounds from the wall and lies, bruised and unconscious, on the ground. Turn to **253**.

331

Another pellet explodes. Deduct 3 points from your STAMINA. The bandit leaps forward, scimitar in hand. Turn to **343**.

332

You outdistance the blob and reach a transit cylinder at the other end of the hall. However, when you enter it you are confronted by an axe-wielding humanoid who has been driven insane and now believes you to be one of the blobs! You must defend yourself against his attack.

INSANE CREWMAN   SKILL 5   STAMINA 6

If you win, turn to **390**.

333

Several hours later, you approach a high tower overshadowing the causeway. Marsatu explains: 'Within the tower is a large, circular platform, called the Roundabout. It consists of a central disc and three rotating rings. If the rings are turned in the proper sequence and thus activated, we can be transported to anywhere on Aarok – even to the Dome of Marvels. It is the only way we can reach the dome, but I fear we will encounter some trouble. You see, only one person knows how to operate the rings, and that is . . .' 'Giant Jym Ego!' booms a mighty voice. From the tower a mighty man storms out, fifteen feet tall with plaited hair and a curly red beard. 'And *I* am he. I've been expecting you both. How fare you, Marsatu? I haven't seen you for some time. I'm afraid the toll's risen again, so I hope you both have large purses and generous dispositions. I've got expensive tastes. Ha, ha!' Legend has it that the Roundabout was built long ago, to ensure that

Aarok's enemies could never reach the defence centre. At that time, the Roundabout could be controlled only by its maker, a giant who collected a small toll for his work. Before he died, he passed its secrets on to his eldest son, who then became its operator. The tradition has been retained, with control passed from father to son, for thousands of years. Three hundred years ago, when Aarok was abandoned, the Roundabout's operator decided to remain behind. Now his great-great-grandson, giant Jym Ego, is in control. But Jym is boisterous and greedy, a thoroughly despicable character . . . 'Well, how much do you have?' yells Jym. Of course, Marsatu took all your credits when he offered to act as your guide. Now what will you do: ask Marsatu for some money to pay your toll (turn to 168), attempt to sweet-talk Jym into providing you with a free trip (turn to 195), or fight him and try to operate the Roundabout yourself (turn to 67)?

334

The old man winks and mumbles, 'Good for ya'! Bet ya' one for it t'night, an' bet the answer's forty-two, ya' not. Have a dart at th' Deik when it's time, ha!' He slips you a tiny dart-gun. (Add this to your *Adventure Sheet*.) While you are pondering his words, he pushes you from your pit and takes it over. Not wishing to argue, will you move towards the brass gong (turn to 214), or examine the candle (turn to 365)?

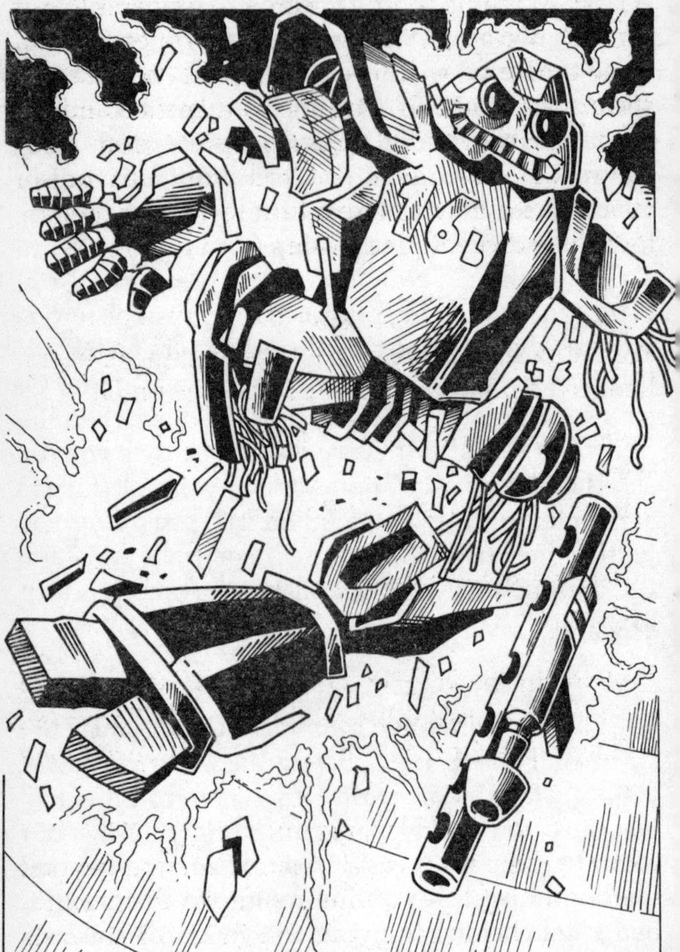

335

A large, grinning robot appears and prepares to exit through two large doors which swivel open for him. Unfortunately, at this moment the bell-craft is struck by a laser bolt. The doors are melted and the robot disintegrates. Deduct 3 points from your STAMINA. Now, will you order an area pulser attack on the enemy ships (turn to **198**), or prepare for a deep dive into the swamp (turn to **37**)?

336

Your port retro is torn by a low-power tractor beam. Reduce your SHIELDS by 1 point *permanently*.

Starspray: Pitch +36.5 . . . Roll +52 . . .
Yaw +6.5 . . .
Enemy: Pitch +35 . . . Roll +60 . . .
Yaw +13 . . .
Relative speed 2000 . . .

You may:

Maintain speed, yaw +10	Turn to **217**
Maintain speed, roll +50	Turn to **82**
Halve speed, pitch +50	Turn to **112**

337

Marsatu, squatting beside you, is peering beyond the dome's steeply curving rooftop to the ground, half a mile below. But your two mechanical beasts have not appeared, and you strongly suspect Jym of thievery. Marsatu is certain of Jym's guilt. 'Swindled by that gigantic gas-bag!' he wheezes. 'He'll pay for his insolence. I'll have him flayed skinless by a ten-tailed prickle-puss! But first, to our business. Down there, ' Marsatu points, 'is the entrance. I'll meet you down there.' Pulling on a pair of magnetic boots, Marsatu runs down the sloping sides of the dome. He has left you stranded. How will you get down? You examine the two spheres Marsatu gave you earlier. If you have brought them with you, you may now wish to use the sphere containing the drill-helmet (turn to 4), the jet boots (turn to 156), or power-gauntlets (turn to 46). If you have none of these items, or do not wish to use them, turn to 196.

338
Just in time, your grabber leaps out and snatches the key from the Deik's hull. Opening your hatch, you swim to the safety of the shore, while both spheres sink rapidly to the bottom of the lake. You have won! Turn to 222.

339
As you turn and run, laser bolts flash by. The bubble-cars are beginning to catch up when you notice a small opening in the wall ahead. Diving through, you find yourself in a small room. Green steam and gas cover the floor. Sitting on a throne before you is a huge, bulb-headed green monster, chewing a tentacle. Looking up, it presses a stud on its chair, and a gate falls down, blocking your escape. 'I seldom have the opportunity of eating a victim alive in my own home!' it says. It holds aloft a small titanium cube, which it rolls. Roll one die. If

you roll 1, 2, 3 or 4, turn to **39**; if you roll 5 or 6, turn to **66**.

340

Several devices now attract your attention. You may examine a multi-armed robot, hanging on a wall (turn to **304**); a small, transparent hemisphere, no larger than your hand (turn to **149**); or an unmarked wooden box (turn to **255**).

341

Krill continues: 'Schaine landed her ship on Lake Droog, where it still resides. She brought an army of mutants with her, which have killed or enslaved many of my people. Still more have been transmuted into evil creatures by a complex biochemical process. Those of us remaining fled to these secret caves. We have been powerless to stop her – until now, that is!' Krill reaches for the high-tech curio of rods, tubes and cubes which the droid had brought back to the cave. 'Schaine's main power, of course, is her mighty spaceship-fortress, from which she launches her assaults. But this device, an interferometer, will temporarily immobilize it, and allow us to attack. My droid was bringing it to this planet when he was attacked by Pelhon Rangers. He tells me that you rescued him, and I am indeed grateful. So what do you desire? I may be able to help.' You tell Krill about your mission, and that you require a spacecraft to reach Aarok. 'That is easy! A backwards time-loop, with half a twist, should do the trick! You shall get your own spaceship back!'

He disappears into a nearby apartment for a few minutes. Roll one die. If you roll 1 or 2, turn to **33**; otherwise, turn to **91**.

342

A mighty roar just behind *Starspray* buffets you towards the Valioog mothership. Reduce your SHIELDS by 1 point *permanently*, and deduct 1 point from your STAMINA. Now, will you try your anti-detector defences (turn to **70**); select the image intensifier scanscope (turn to **215**); or risk activating the atomic polarizer (turn to **90**)?

343

You attack the bandit with your javelin.

BANDIT   SKILL 7   STAMINA 8

If you win, turn to **293**.

344

At dusk you stumble into a tiny hamlet of clay and stone buildings. The ramshackle bungalows and two-storey villas are in a bad state: the village has been deserted for some time. But at least you can guess, by the style of building, that the inhabitants must have been humanoid. Marching through the village, you come to a sign-post. Will you continue along Spitflak's Street (turn to **394**), or turn left into Winsome's Way (turn to **204**)?

345

You decide to turn the red ring one segment clockwise, then your phase ends. Glip turns the red ring one segment anti-clockwise, but his path to you is blocked by a screen, so his phase ends. Scuttlebug rotates the blue ring one segment clockwise, and his phase ends. Finally Mutant rotates the yellow ring one segment anti-clockwise. He can see you at the end of his phase, so he charges across the rings to attack. You begin swivelling the laser-cannon attached to your mechanical beast towards him, but you are too late. He is upon you and you must fight hand-to-claw.

| YELLOW MUTANT | SKILL 7 | STAMINA 8 |

If you win, another Mutant appears on the vacated spot on the red ring. The second move begins. Will you turn the red ring one segment clockwise (turn to **250**), or two segments anti-clockwise (turn to **150**)?

346
You have just made a terrible mistake! The weed spreads rapidly and fouls your huge starboard thruster. Both the *Starspray* and yourself are blown to pieces.

347
Unluckily, you are baked by a powerful gamma-beam.

348
On a radarscope, you watch an enemy blip to the south disappear from the screen. But simultaneously the speaker blares out, 'Danger! Incoming missile . . .' There is a mighty blast, blowing the bell and yourself to pieces.

349

As the figure approaches, he appears to shrink considerably and grow wider in the girth. What you mistook for a tall, dark, sinister figure was only this man's shadow, cast by his lantern's light. Now looking up at you is a dumpy old man with thick, pursed lips, drooping eyelids and a balding pate. Like yourself, he has four arms, which are wrapped snugly into the folds of a voluminous green habit. His footsteps are cushioned by his fluffy orange moccasins. 'Hail, stranger, and welcome!' he exalts, raising a pudgy hand. 'All is fine! A most enchanting evening is before us, is it not? But I see that you are weary. You have had many struggles, yes?' He peers a little closer: 'I have a special remedy to cure *all* your troubles. Yes, indeed! Perhaps you will join me for refreshment – my home is not far away.' If you wish to avail yourself of his generosity, turn to **5**; if you wish to travel on alone, turn to **395**.

350

All the square-shaped tiles change colour: orange to green, green to blue, blue to orange. You now have no option but to step on tile E3; the circles now change colour: orange to green, green to blue, blue to orange. Now will you step on tile E4 (turn to **372**), or tile D3 (turn to **321**)?

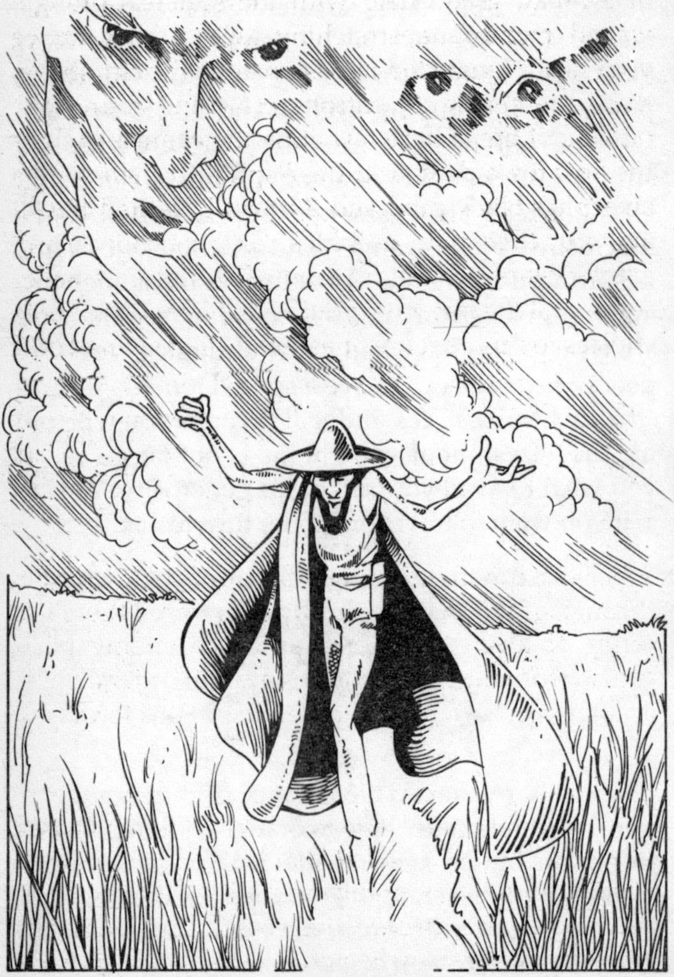

351

The sphere is a skew-dimensional container, warping volume. Within it, you appear minute, standing in a broad green field with the sphere's orange-walled membrane stretching away, miles above your head. Huge dim faces appear in the sky above; these are the inn's patrons crowding round the outside of the sphere, awaiting the contest. Across the field towards you strides a sprightly man, with a sweeping black cape and a broad-brimmed hat. 'I am your first trial,' he states. 'Tell me, how many greater stars orbit the plane of destiny? Answer true, or I'll obliterate you!' He offers you three choices to this obscure question. Will you answer:

42?	Turn to 42
65?	Turn to 65
384?	Turn to 384

352

A heavily armed, grinning robot appears, then exits through a large hatch. Shortly afterwards there is a series of loud explosions, and two enemy blips vanish from the radarscope. Now you order a missile attack on two more enemy ships. Turn to 198.

353

Your ship is a ridiculous contraption: all popped rivets and buckled plates, and leaking like a sieve. Crouching uncomfortably behind the tiny wheelhouse, you manoeuvre the vessel, and yourself, into deep water. Slowly, and in jerks, you approach the enemy craft: a sleek white cutter bristling with lasers – not at all what you had expected. Your chances appear slim. Will you fire a salvo into her starboard side (turn to **146**), or steam at full speed across her bow (turn to **170**)?

354

You follow a trail over a ridge and on for perhaps a quarter of a mile. Now, ahead, you can see the droid again: he has been waylaid by a green mutant with arms extending from its cheeks and thighs. You decide to attack it and rescue the droid.

GREEN MUTANT   SKILL 7   STAMINA 6

If you win, turn to **76**.

355

The book contains a booby-trap. When you open it, you detonate a small explosive device – just enough to give you a nasty shock. Deduct 2 points from your STAMINA. You may now remove a book you had not previously taken down:

Relative Non-Relativity	Turn to **104**
Baba's Book of Homemade Wines	Turn to **305**

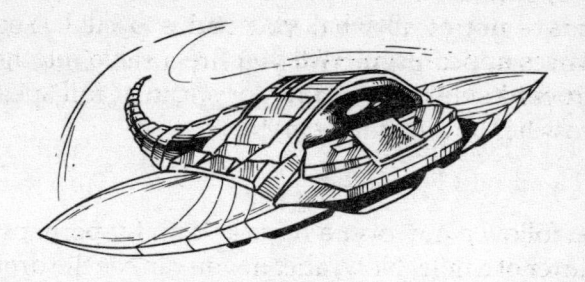

356

You take the warder's needle-gun. Increase your SKILL by 1 point. When you turn towards L'Bastin, you see that he is dying, shot by a stray needle during your struggle. 'Take the passage left, and down the air-tube to Vault 7,' he directs. 'There you will find my laboratory and the vats. Add the salt to the mixture.' He coughs and whispers faintly, 'One more thing I would like you to know. The Prefectas, even properly constructed, are not the perfect lifeform. They are excellent warriors – nothing more. You see, I did find out, through my experiments, what the perfect organism is. They already exist – in the natural environment. But they weren't suitable for my plans of conquest. You see, they are . . .' He forces out a final word. *No!* They can't be *that*! Surely not! Well, what does it matter anyway. L'Bastin closes his eyes and departs from the 3rd dimension. It is time for you to leave also. Following L'Bastin's instructions, you creep along the passage towards the air-tube. *Test your Luck*. If you are Lucky, turn to **276**; if you are Unlucky, turn to **388**.

357

Reduce your oxygen supply by 2 points. Farkin croaks as you thump him with your weapon. His grip is loosening. Will you:

Try a bear-hug?	Turn to **95**
Head-butt Fog Farkin?	Turn to **268**

358

'Very well,' the speaker whines, 'you have requested manual control of auxiliary combat vehicle BAB-1.' In front of your feet, a metal door suddenly slides open and a tracked vehicle, sporting two lasers and a grabbing crane, rises from the level below. The metal crane seizes you and inserts you into a tiny compartment high up on the machine. Simultaneously two huge iron doors in front swivel open, allowing you to drive the vehicle out of the bell. Revving your combat vehicle, you enter the murky swamp. Turn to **393**.

359

Fog Farkin comes from a rare breed of monsters called Chogs. Though lacking arms, Chogs are very agile and, you recall, have a deadly, natural weapon . . . Like lightning, a flabby, leaf-like tongue powers from Farkin's larynx and glues itself to your face. It is smothering you! You begin the following combat with the ten oxygen supply points shown on your *Adventure Sheet*; you will use up some of these during your fight. *If you use them all up, then you have been suffocated and your adventure is over*. Will you:

Use your strength to break free?	Turn to **180**
Grope for your laser-pistol?	Turn to **131**
Neck-chop Fog Farkin?	Turn to **105**

360

You receive a glancing blow from a magnetic pulverizer. Reduce your SHIELDS by 1 point *permanently*. Now your screens flash:

Starspray: Pitch +1.5 . . . Roll +52 . . .
Yaw −24.5 . . .
Enemy: Pitch +35 . . . Roll +60 . . .
Yaw +13 . . .
Relative speed 2000 . . .

Will you:

Maintain speed and course? Turn to **285**
Maintain speed, pitch +10? Turn to **98**
Increase speed to 4000? Turn to **248**

361

During this move, Glip turns the red circle one segment anti-clockwise and attacks. After a tough encounter you defeat him. Next, Scuttlebug turns the blue ring one segment clockwise, but his path is blocked by a screen. Finally Mutant turns the yellow ring one segment anti-clockwise, attacks, and is defeated. But giant Jym Ego shakes his head. 'That was the fourth and last move of the game. I'm afraid you didn't defeat a Scuttlebug in time. Never mind! So long, and thanks for the entertainment!' Jym pulls a lever, and you are obliterated.

362

You strip a whole row of its delicious contents and eat them greedily. Unfortunately, they had been sprayed with a pesticide, so you have just poisoned yourself! Deduct 3 points from your STAMINA. If you are still alive, you scout around and observe several items lying about which may prove useful later on. Choose two from the following list and add them to your *Adventure Sheet*.

>pot plant
>strawberries
>shovel
>weed-killer
>broom
>plastic hose

When you have chosen, you decide to follow a corridor heading from the hall. Turn to **103**.

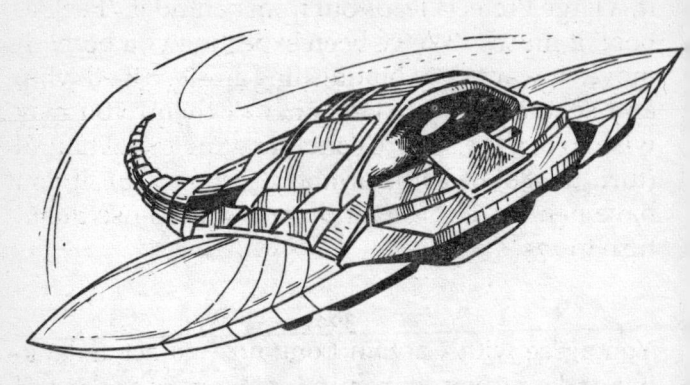

Marsatu guides you through the yawning gateway, into the Dome of Marvels. You are most disappointed. Apart from a solitary egg-shaped obelisk cemented into the floor, the interior is bare. 'Of course,' explains Marsatu, 'this was once a fabulous place, filled with the wonders of the galaxy. Some of the most famous artists in the universe performed here. It was here that Madame Du Braggit, the renowned comedian and political satirist, recited her 'Greatest Joke of the Universe' before Aarok's king and high nobility. Unfortunately the king construed Madame Du Braggit's joke as being a slur against himself – and of course you know the rest of the story. It is said that her headless ghost sometimes wanders into the dome, laughing hysterically, though why she should do so, or even *how* for that matter, is beyond me!' Marsatu now points towards the obelisk. 'That is the way to Vault 6, and the defence centre. Your mission is almost at its end!' You both approach the obelisk, but just as you reach it, a large Prefecta leaps out from behind it. 'Peek-a-boo!' it muses. 'We've been expecting you both!' It moves towards you brandishing an electrified whip and scythe. If you have either of them, you may wish to use the sphere containing the metal hound (turn to **288**) or battle-armour (turn to **246**). If you have neither of these, or do not wish to use them, turn to **275**.

364

You agree with Captain Long-nose to act as lookout and air sailor, in return for a voyage to Central City, where he intends to make repairs to his ship. The barge takes off and, at a height of fifty feet, cruises towards the city walls. After a few hours, you notice another ship approaching at speed from the south. It is the barge of Captain Big-ears, your captain's rival. Roll one die. If you roll a 1, turn to **329**; if you roll 2 or 3, turn to **286**; if you roll 4 or 5, turn to **249**; if you roll a 6, turn to **172**.

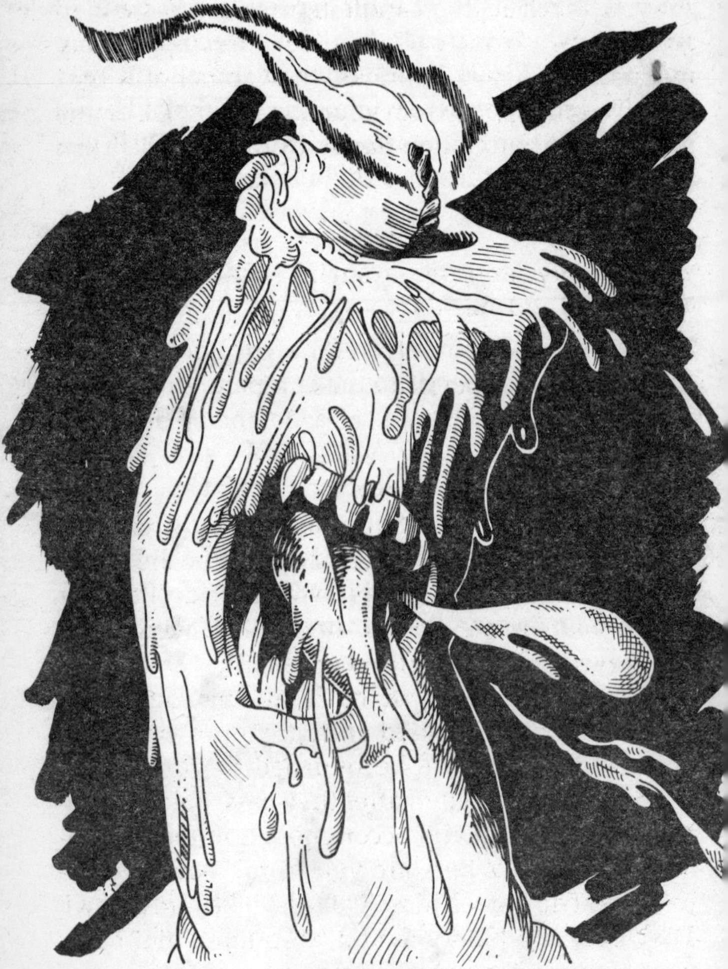

365

As you touch it, the candle-figure screams out in annoyance. 'You oaf! You've interrupted my meditation!' Again it shrieks, then spits hot wax at you. Deduct 1 point from your STAMINA. All of this unexpected commotion has awoken the Deik. Turn to 10.

366

Your enemy launches a smart missile, complete with lasers and shields.

SMART
 MISSILE   RATING 8   LASERS 2   SHIELDS 4

If you win, turn to 231.

367

You are dragged into the room you had first seen through the window, where the man in the white suit introduces himself as Woderwick. 'Perhaps you've heard of me – er, us,' he says, glancing at the three-eyed cat who has been silently examining you. Woderwick tells you that he and his cohorts are a band of 'liberal-minded entrepreneurs' (meaning pirates); that you will be returned to your family shortly, intact (mostly), after they have paid a 'modest transportation and accommodation fee', meaning a ransom. 'Where are you from?' asks Woderwick. You do not tell him. 'Guards, take him below!' They beat and bind you and, through a dim haze, you are aware that you are being dragged into one of the tetrahedrons near the mansion. Then you black out. Turn to 237.

368

The computer asks you to verify that you have selected plan 368, which you do. 'Very well,' it drones, 'you have requested the "take 'em all with you" plan: annihilation of all craft within a fifty-mile radius, using a ten-megaton bomb. Goodbye, cruel world!' You are obliterated.

369

The *Starspray* is punctured by many thousands of needle-like shards of a scintillating metal, released from the Valioog ship. Reduce your SHIELDS by 1 point *permanently*, and deduct 2 points from your STAMINA. Roaring away, will you now prefer to operate an electro-magnetic scanscope (turn to **215**); switch off your Gauss Pandimonializer (turn to **389**); or push the flashing orange button on your console (turn to **342**)?

370

The captain yells a spate of abuse at you, before steering his craft away. Turn to **32**.

371

When you touch a plastic spigot, both it and the brass hoop to which it was attached dissolve, enabling you to exit the passage either to right (turn to 242), or to left (turn to 274), or you may continue along the passage towards the farther exit left (turn to 257).

372

The electrodes of both ships become entwined. By the time they have unravelled, you are both badly hurt. Deduct 4 points from your STAMINA. If you are still alive, you may:

Pull out a crystal knob	Turn to 291
Stamp your foot on a floor-plate	Turn to 314

373

You blast the pillar to pieces; unfortunately, you kill the creature you were trying to help, in the process. You shrug and turn back up the passage, as there is no other exit from the cavern. Turn to 140.

374

After a while, the rather paunchy guard crawls over to you and prods your cocoon. Many of his bright clustered eyes have been blackened; strangely, these resemble the imprint of a boot heel! 'Garn! I'll make you suffer, you ugly, four-armed thing!' it hisses, shaking you and banging your head with a rock. Deduct 1 point from your STAMINA. Will you answer him rudely (turn to 147), or pretend you have been killed by his blow (turn to 138)?

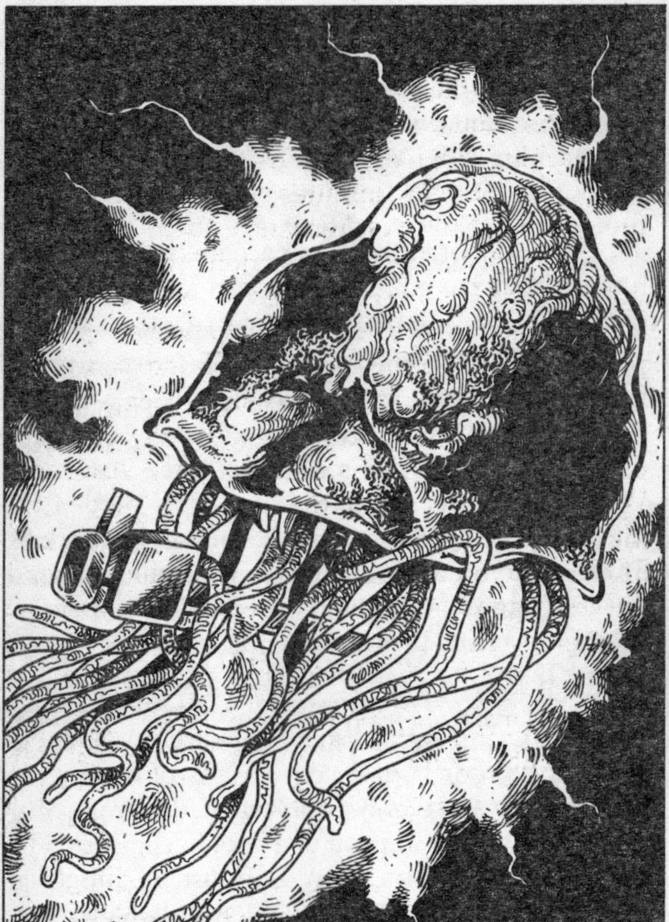

375

The bluff gradually melts into a broad plain of black earth, crazed with streams of whites, yellows, greens and blues. You wander on for a little, but soon you become lost in the falling darkness. At the same time, you notice three small luminous globes approaching from the eastern skies. These hover above you for a few minutes before descending to the ground. Now you recognize them – they are cosmic jellyfish; you are in serious trouble! 'Hey, gringo!' the fluorescent golden one calls out. 'Haven't we met before, on another planet, perhaps?' 'Si, si!' pipes up a second one, sporting a leather bandolier and a six-shot mega-blaster. 'You're Jang Mistral! You busted us for Turdleburder rustlin' on Wayliff's Asteroid three years ago! We spent eighteen months in a tiny, nettle-tick-infested gaol for that, so now you're gonna pay!' These dudes mean business! You must defend yourself as best you can.

	SKILL	STAMINA
KILLER KRUN	9	6
NOADO THE BANDIT	8	4
RUTHLESS ROD	6	6

If you win, turn to **271**.

376

For a long time you struggle over the purple dunes, baking under the blazing star of Sev. When evening arrives, you are still a long march away from the city walls. Near by, a cluster of flat-topped pillars, arranged in a rough circle, jut from the desert floor; you are determined to camp there for the night. But when you arrive, you hear a peculiar, low-pitched gabbling: a pack of desert creatures, or mutants, must have smelt you from the surrounding dunes. You may wish to climb one of the pillars for safety (turn to 281), or you could try to sneak quietly away (turn to 31).

377

In the afternoon you trek onwards, over massive tumbling dunes, through troughs of sand and ash, along rocky desert valleys. Standing on a dune, you notice two large air-barges, skimming frantically across the desert, engaged in combat. Eventually one barge breaks away, trailing smoke and flames. The other barge is quite close. Will you wave at it to attract attention (turn to 186), or do you prefer to hide and wait until it passes (turn to 32)?

378

From a distance, you see the bell-craft being torn to pieces, and then sink into the swamp. Several small enemy craft are approaching your combat vehicle, which has been badly damaged. But luckily, the city is not very far away, perhaps two miles. Even closer than this, however, is a concrete launch wharf with a hover-ship moored alongside, and a tubeway terminal building. You steer your vehicle towards them. *Test your Luck*. If you are Lucky, turn to 169; if you are Unlucky, turn to 235.

379

You enter a long, low compartment filled with heavy throbbing equipment; it is the station's pulser-drive engine-room. Behind you trundles the blob, which now forms itself into a sub-human shape and continues to chase after you. You flee along the hall towards a transit cylinder. During this headlong pursuit, you observe a number of artefacts lying around. You may snatch up two items, which you hope will come in useful later on, from the following list.

> wrench
> hammer
> sonic screwdriver
> fire extinguisher
> multifacetous aciduator
> ball-bearings

When you have decided which two you require, add them to your *Adventure Sheet*, then turn to **332**.

380

In one villa you are investigating you are assaulted by a jump-pole: a peculiar creature resembling a wooden stick, common to many planets. The mischievous jump-pole, catching you unawares, gives you a sound clout behind the ears. Deduct 3 points from your STAMINA. Unfortunately for the creature, you are quicker than it had anticipated. As it bounds towards the door, you leap after it and seize it in all four hands. Its expression changes from one of mischievous glee to absolute terror. 'Gahgo!

Aagi!' it creaks as you clumsily apply too much pressure and break it in half. A pity! Jump-poles are very knowledgeable, and this one could have provided you with a great deal of valuable information. With little else of interest in the village, you now leave via Spitflak's Street, using half of the jump-pole as a short staff! Turn to **160**.

381

'What!' exclaims the toad, grabbing at the bag of pellets. During your tussle, you drop the pouch. The pellets detonate, there is a terrific roar, and you are both consumed in a huge ball of fire.

382

You pass through the ovoid air-lock and remove your helmet. The air contains the faintest whiff of rocket fuel. There is a leak, so you must be careful not to use your laser sword or pistol here, for fear of sparking an explosion. Ahead of you is a long passage of gently tapering hoops. Attached to many hoops are strange spigots of glass or plastic. Further along the passage is an exit to the left. You may walk along the passage towards the exit (turn to **257**), or examine a glass spigot (turn to **245**), or a plastic spigot (turn to **371**).

383

You have badly misjudged, and slam into a massive revolving pylon of the *Grand Archipelago*.

384

'A false reply, heretic!' The old man raises a finger and blasts you into oblivion.

385

You re-enter the study, then, walking through several walls, find yourself in the mansion's old-fashioned kitchen. Here, you disturb a grumpy, boil-nosed chef, who drops a newly baked soufflé in his surprise. The ill-tempered creature grabs a laser-carver and, using a large pot as a shield, rounds on you.

	RATING	LASERS	SHIELDS
CHEF	5	2	8
YOUR POLYARMOUR	–	2	10

If you win, you must discard the polyarmour, as its power is draining and you are finding it difficult to move. Turn to **284**.

386

A stale yellow gas hisses from the air-seal, but the hatch will not budge. You may twist the handles in any combination you have not yet tried – either:

Turn red and blue handles clockwise	Turn to **93**
Turn red and blue anti-clockwise	Turn to **118**
Turn red anti-clockwise, blue clockwise	Turn to **192**

387

'Thank you!' cries the creature you have just saved. It is extremely grateful, and gives you one of its possessions – a sensory capsule, which it tells you to insert into your back teeth. 'It may help you escape from a tricky situation,' the beast tells you before departing. (Add the sensory capsule to your *Adventure Sheet*.) Now you return along the passage, as there is no other exit from the cavern. Turn to **140**.

388

Near the air-tube, you are attacked by one of L'Bastin's roaming pets: a gigantic fanged armadillo-bodied rhinoceros.

MUTATED RHINO   SKILL 7   STAMINA 8

If you win, turn to **276**.

389

In an instant, you are blasted to atoms by a mighty nuclear explosion.

390

You leave the transit cylinder and enter a bubble-shaped dome. About you are computer terminals, consoles, scanscopes and the like, all clicking noisily and flashing in some deranged manner. Clumsily you rest your elbow on a green button, causing a speaker to announce: 'Alert, alert! Unauthorized intruder! Cyborg anti-intruder defences activated!' Steam whistles from several holes in the console, badly scalding you. Deduct 3 points from your

STAMINA. You hear the metallic pounding of a cyborg's feet, approaching the dome. You decide hastily to exit through a hatch on the opposite side of the dome. Will you pass through a round hatch (turn to **9**), or a square hatch (turn to **167**)?

391

In the heat of the afternoon, the spider curls up to sleep. Fortuitously you have noticed, projecting from the nearest cocoon, a number of long, sharp quills, belonging to the luckless creature within. You also have a few fingers poking from a small hole in your cocoon so, swinging yourself across, you manage to grab a quill. Will you break its tip off (turn to **157**) or snap it off at its base (turn to **133**)?

392

Climbing down a ladder, you enter the next level of the ship. Within it are many machines and craft, some still boxed up in large wooden crates. But behind one crate, you encounter a grim little robotoid who stares blandly at you, declaring: 'Sorry mate, you have no authorization!' He whirls forward to attack.

LITTLE ROBOTOID   SKILL 6   STAMINA 8

If you win, turn to **340**.

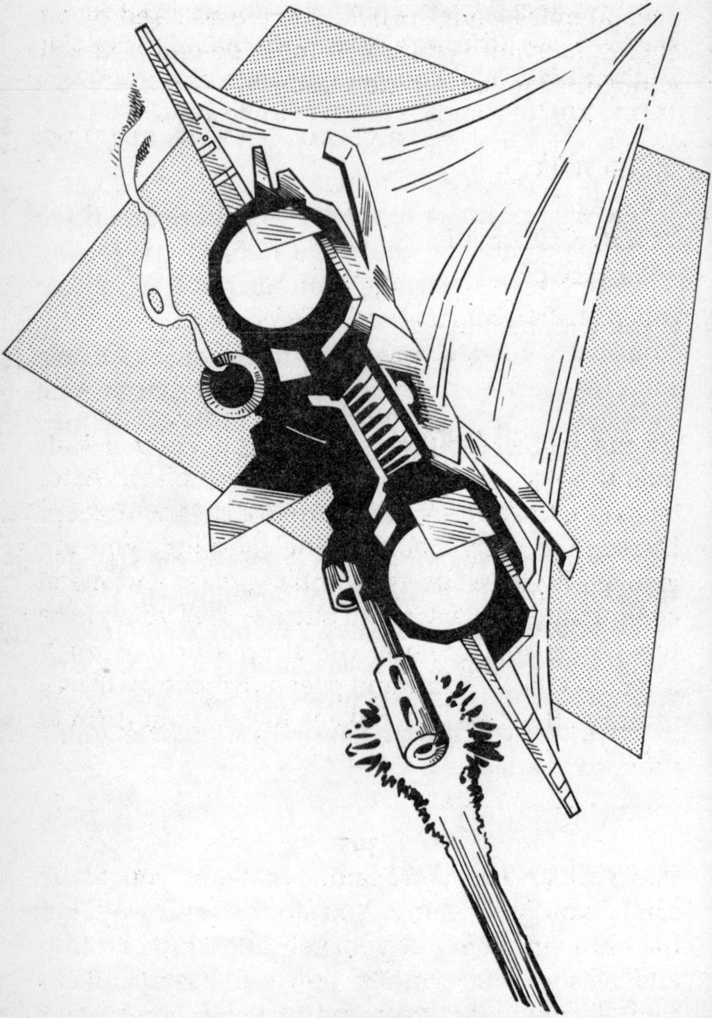

393

Several miles from the bell, you are attacked by an enemy mosquito-craft. You must defend yourself with your combat vehicle's lasers.

	RATING	LASERS	SHIELDS
MOSQUITO-CRAFT	4	4	8
YOUR COMBAT VEHICLE	–	2	10

If you win, turn to 378.

394

At the end of Spitflak's Street you enter a hut, intending to spend the night in comfort. After fastening the door, you curl up in a corner to sleep. During the early hours of the morning, you are awoken by the sounds of tinkling glass and metal coming from the pavement outside. Will you ignore the noise and go back to sleep (turn to 295), approach the window and peer outside (turn to 55), or unbar the door and poke your head out (turn to 108)?

395

The old man asks you again. 'No, thank you all the same,' you reply stiffly. You step on your way, but the old man, angry at your refusal, whirls around and slashes you with a powerful laser cutlass. Mortally wounded, you fall to the ground, your adventure over.

396

All the squares now change colour: orange to green, green to blue, blue to orange. Will you step on tile C4 (turn to **294**), tile E4 then E5, (turn to **193**), or tile D5 (turn to **110**)?

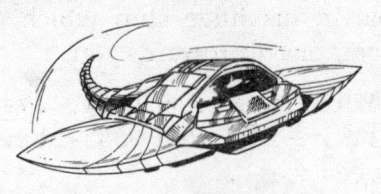

397

You are attacked by a tubeway guard and a number of ill-tempered dignitaries who have congregated near the gates.

	SKILL	STAMINA
LION-MASKED GUARD	8	6
HOOK-NOSED DIGNITARY	6	4
FOPPISH DIGNITARY	6	6

If you win, roll one die. If you roll 1, 2, 3 or 4, turn to **262**; if you roll 5 or 6, turn to **145**.

398

Through a small hole in the side of the sphere, you fire a dart. Well aimed, it pierces both your opponent's ship and his shell. The Deik shrieks and drops, stunned. Manipulating your controls, you manage to grab your key from the enemy sphere, then open your hatch and swim to the safety of the shore. You are just in time to see both spheres sink beneath the waves. You have won! Turn to **222**.

399

Your laser fire cuts through the enemy's shields and burns a hole in his huge ship which, spurting smoke, lumbers angrily towards you.

Starspray: Pitch +34 ... Roll +142 ... Yaw 0 ...
Enemy: Pitch +35 ... Roll +60 ... Yaw +13 ...
Relative speed 1000 ...

You may:

Accelerate to 2000, pitch +30, roll +60, yaw +5	Turn to **269**
Maintain speed, pitch +47.5, roll +90, yaw −6.5	Turn to **112**
Halve speed, pitch +60, roll +60, yaw +5	Turn to **312**

400

And so your mission ends successfully; single-handed, you have saved the galaxy! After several minor adventures, you reach the surface of Aarok and, piloting a disused spaceship, return to Ensulina. Several months later, when Aarok has been decontaminated and set in order, you return there at the head of a large colonizing fleet. In the Dome of Marvels, the Grand Emperor himself will crown you – galactic superhero, and first ruler of New Aarok. Soon, you will begin a long and just reign over a billion people ...